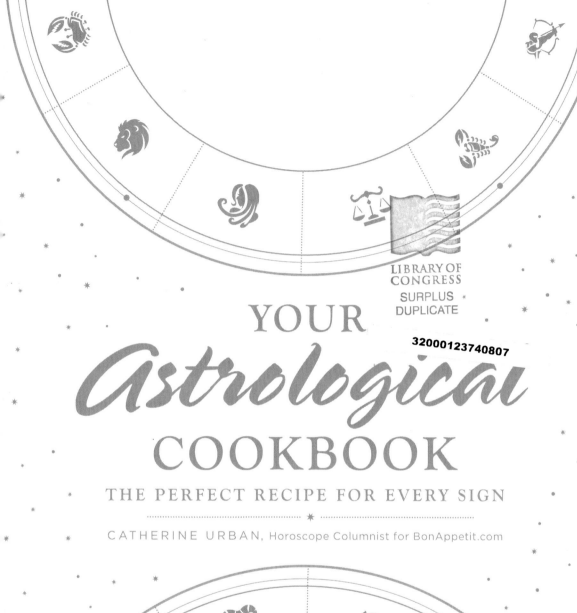

YOUR
Astrological
COOKBOOK

THE PERFECT RECIPE FOR EVERY SIGN

CATHERINE URBAN, Horoscope Columnist for BonAppetit.com

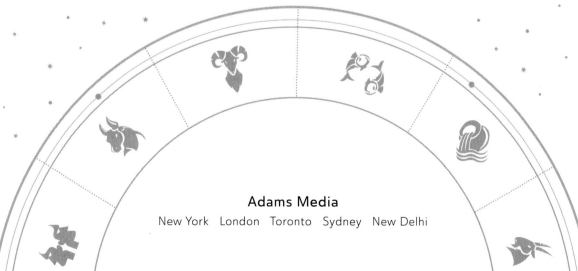

Adams Media
New York   London   Toronto   Sydney   New Delhi

Adams Media
An Imprint of Simon & Schuster, Inc.
57 Littlefield Street
Avon, Massachusetts 02322

First Adams Media hardcover edition November 2019

ADAMS MEDIA and colophon are trademarks of Simon & Schuster.

For information about special discounts for bulk purchases, please contact Simon & Schuster Special Sales at 1-866-506-1949 or business@simonandschuster.com.

The Simon & Schuster Speakers Bureau can bring authors to your live event. For more information or to book an event contact the Simon & Schuster Speakers Bureau at 1-866-248-3049 or visit our website at www.simonspeakers.com.

Interior design by Sylvia McArdle
Photographs by Harper Point Photography
Illustrations © 123RF/PremiumDesign

Manufactured in the United States of America

10 9 8 7 6 5 4 3 2 1

Library of Congress Cataloging-in-Publication Data
Names: Urban, Catherine, author.
Title: Your astrological cookbook / Catherine Urban, horoscope columnist for BonAppetit.com.
Description: Avon, Massachusetts: Adams Media, 2019.
Identifiers: LCCN 2019023189 | ISBN 9781507211113 (hc) | ISBN 9781507211120 (ebook)
Subjects: LCSH: Cooking. | Astrology. | LCGFT: Cookbooks.
Classification: LCC TX652 .U73 2019 | DDC 641.5--dc23
LC record available at https://lccn.loc.gov/2019023189

ISBN 978-1-5072-1111-3
ISBN 978-1-5072-1112-0 (ebook)

Always follow safety and commonsense cooking protocols while using kitchen utensils, operating ovens and stoves, and handling uncooked food. If children are assisting in the preparation of any recipe, they should always be supervised by an adult.

Contains material adapted from the following titles published by Adams Media, an Imprint of Simon & Schuster, Inc.:

The Everything® Bartender's Book, 4th Edition by Cheryl Charming, copyright © 2015, ISBN: 978-1-4405-8633-0.

The Everything® Easy Asian Cookbook by Kelly Jaggers, copyright © 2015, ISBN: 978-1-4405-9016-0.

The Everything® Easy Italian Cookbook by Dawn Altomari, copyright © 2015, ISBN: 978-1-4405-8533-3.

The Everything® Easy Mediterranean Cookbook by Peter Minaki, copyright © 2015, ISBN: 978-1-4405-9240-9.

The Everything® Easy Mexican Cookbook by Margaret Kaeter and Linda Larsen, copyright © 2015, ISBN: 978-1-4405-8716-0.

The Everything® Easy Vegetarian Cookbook by Jay Weinstein, copyright © 2015, ISBN: 978-1-4405-8719-1.

The Everything® Giant Book of Juicing by Teresa Kennedy, copyright © 2013, ISBN: 978-1-4405-5785-9.

The Everything® Healthy College Cookbook by Nicole Cormier, RD, copyright © 2010, ISBN: 978-1-4405-0411-2.

The Everything® Healthy Cooking for Parties Book by Linda Larsen, copyright © 2008, ISBN: 978-1-59869-925-8.

The Everything® Whole Foods Cookbook by Rachel Rappaport, copyright © 2012, ISBN: 978-1-4405-3168-2.

Dedication

For my love, Eli. Immense gratitude goes out to the families on both sides who have passed down their culinary traditions and signature dishes. (Glad we finally have a table large enough to seat everyone!) And finally, big thanks to Alex Beggs for her guidance in combining writing, food, and astrology.

CONTENTS

Taurus:
The Smooth Chef   40

Gemini:
The Adventurous Chef   62

Cancer:

The Mood Chef   84

Leo:

The Luminous Chef   107

Virgo:
The Logical Chef 128

Libra:
The Fancy Chef 149

Scorpio:
The Enigmatic Chef 170

Sagittarius:
The Innovator Chef 192

Capricorn:
The Sophisticated Chef   214

Aquarius:
The Scientist Chef   235

Pisces:

The Intuitive Chef   256

Introduction

Are you a passionate Sagittarius looking for a meal to warm your heart? A serious Capricorn looking for simple dishes with ingredients you trust? A balanced Libra looking for food that is both healthy and fun? Whether you're hosting a party, sharing a meal with a close friend, or simply looking for some cooking inspiration for yourself, *Your Astrological Cookbook* will help you find the perfect meal and drink for any occasion—all determined by your astrological sign!

You probably check your horoscope to learn more about your love life, career, or financial outlook—and that same convention can work for food too! Each astrological sign has food favorites based on their personality traits, ranging from the aesthetic appeal, to the flavors, and even to the origins of the food itself. By tapping into the tastes and traits of your zodiac sign, you can reveal the perfect meal for you.

Not sure where to start? Fortunately, *Your Astrological Cookbook* has done all the legwork for you by designing a full menu for your sign (and everyone else at your table!) so that all you have to do is cook, eat, and enjoy!

This book is divided into thirteen chapters with more than two hundred carefully chosen food and drink recipes. In the first chapter, Stellar Dishes, you'll learn about cooking for your element and your modality, and what types of food appeal to which elemental signs. Each of the remaining twelve chapters is devoted entirely to one astrological sign, where you'll find everything from the sign's personality quirks to a variety of recipes that align with the distinct preferences of that sign. For example: Are you a luxury-loving Taurus? Try some Fig, Prosciutto, and Brie Bruschetta. Are you hosting a party for a fiery Leo? Try Chickpeas in Potato and Onion Curry. Are you a nostalgic Cancer? Make some homemade Chicken Potpie.

No matter what your sign, you'll discover new and exciting dimensions through the delicious and creative path of food—breakfast, lunch, dinner, party foods, and everything else in between, all crafted with an astrological twist!

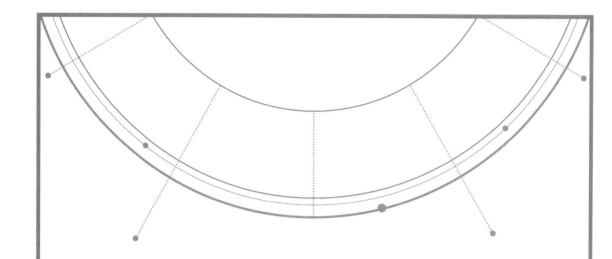

Stellar Dishes:
Combining Astrology and Cooking

The Sun represents your individuality and describes how you shine in the world. Your "Sun sign" is also known as your "zodiac sign," or even as casually as "your sign." Most people know their Sun sign, because it is one of the most important personality barometers in astrology. The Sun represents the essence of who you are. So naturally, the recipes specially chosen for your sign are dishes that will complement you as well as peanut butter complements jelly!

But don't stop there! This book will also walk you through how you can satisfy your Moon sign or even your Venus sign. And don't forget about your elemental family. The other signs in your elemental family will feature stellar recipes guaranteed to get your tummy rumbling, so don't be shy! Similarly, you might like to explore the recipes of the signs that share your sign's modality, which sets your sign's pace. Still want more? Impress your friends and family by inviting them over and tailoring a starry evening menu to their sign's taste. Or you can even plan your meals around the Sun's or Moon's current zodiac sign. Let's learn how!

Your Sign's Makeup

Each of the twelve signs has an elemental classification, sharing a resonance with either fire, earth, air, or water. With three signs attributed to each element, these elemental groupings are known as "triplicities." Broken down even further, each of those three signs also has its own modality—cardinal, fixed, or mutable. The element gives a quality to the sign, while the modality sets the pace, resulting in a unique celestial signature attributed to each zodiac sign. Take a look at the following grid to find your elemental grouping and modality.

ELEMENT-MODE GRID				
	Fire	**Earth**	**Air**	**Water**
Cardinal	Aries	Capricorn	Libra	Cancer
Fixed	Leo	Taurus	Aquarius	Scorpio
Mutable	Sagittarius	Virgo	Gemini	Pisces

Eat by Element

Think of the signs sharing your element as your cosmic BFFs. You have a lot in common, and you feel comfortable around one another. So pull up a seat at their table! Any Virgo will sense a familiarity with fellow earth signs Taurus and Capricorn. Are you a watery Cancer? Paddle over to see what Scorpio and Pisces are cooking up!

FIRE SIGNS

Aries, Leo, and Sagittarius, you belong to the fire element. Passionate, warm, and full of life, you follow what excites you. Fire natives really know how to bring the heat! With big personalities and a contagious glow, you bring the life to the party. Fire signs are likeable, fun, and energizing to be around. You prefer excitement and will pass on anything bland. Your recipes veer on the vibrant side, just like your personality!

EARTH SIGNS

Taurus, Virgo, and Capricorn, your element is earth. Grounded, practical, and industrious, your domain is the material world. If it weren't for you, the world would be a very chaotic place. You are contained, which lets everyone know they can count on you. Organization is a virtue, and you are as realistic as they come. Did we mention that you are resourceful? You like recipes that are solid, are not overly complicated, and feature ingredients you can trust.

AIR SIGNS

Gemini, Libra, and Aquarius, you make up the social sector of the zodiac. Air is your element, giving you the freedom to breeze in and out of conversations and trending hashtags. You thrive on intellectual stimulation, a good debate, and random facts. There are few subjects you won't entertain. Entertaining? You're great at that too! And because you love learning, you're game to try new things in the kitchen, which always makes for a fun time!

WATER SIGNS

Cancer, Scorpio, and Pisces, you belong to the water realm. Intuitive, perceptive, dreamy, and sensitive, your feelings are your compass in life. You feel everything intently, and frequently need periods of solitude to find your center. Empathic and compassionate, you are adept at connecting with others. For you, language is often unspoken. Guided by what you feel, you like a dish that speaks to your mood.

Cooking by Modality

The cardinal signs are found at the beginning of each season. Taking initiative and starting projects come naturally to them, though follow-through is not their strong suit. Leave that to the fixed signs! The fixed signs represent the middle of the season, the pure expression of that season. Fixed signs are as steady as they come. They know what they like, and they do not like change. That's where the mutable signs come in. Adaptable, innovative, and a bit unpredictable, the mutable signs are here to stir the pot!

THE CARDINAL SIGNS: ARIES, CANCER, LIBRA, CAPRICORN

Trying a new dish is so exciting! Unafraid to take risks and try new things, you are never disappointed if you don't nail it on the first try. It's all about the experience! Which is why you'll have no problem at all skipping around this book. Cardinal recipes will meet your innate courageousness to brave the unknown. You love introducing others to your culinary discoveries—whether hosting at your place or taking your dish to a party.

THE FIXED SIGNS: TAURUS, LEO, SCORPIO, AQUARIUS

Three words to describe your culinary style? Quality, consistency, and technique. You've got a few signature dishes up your sleeve that you've made time and time again and that repeatedly win everyone over. You like preparing a dish you know is going to be good. Fixed signs understand patience, and since the best things in life are worth waiting for, you'll happily stand by while that slow cooker works its magic.

THE MUTABLE SIGNS: GEMINI, VIRGO, SAGITTARIUS, PISCES

You take life as it comes, which means that you typically don't think about food until hunger strikes. Didn't go grocery shopping? No problem. You're adept at innovating a killer recipe with what's available in the pantry. No cashews? Peanut butter should do the trick! Quick on your toes, you are witty and think fast, which makes for some extraordinarily creative cuisine!

Your Planet's Influence

If you've ever looked at your astrological chart, you'll notice that all twelve signs of the zodiac encompass the wheel and that you have planets in other signs! Each of these planets plays a role in your personality. Let's shine a light on these heavenly spheres at work in the kitchen!

THE MOON: REPLENISH YOURSELF

When you're tired, cranky, or dare we say hangry, your Moon will do the talking. Essentially, your Moon sign describes who you are when you are emotional! When you feel like you don't have your needs met, your Moon influences how you will react and what you need to feel better. We often have an emotional connection to food because when we were babies (and instinct was all we knew), mother's milk was there for us. In fact, the Moon rules milk, our very first form of nutrients!

Yep, the Moon pretty much rules sustenance itself. Fulfilling our Moon's cravings lets our body and mind know that we are cared for. At the end of an exhausting week, what foods do you crave? Your Moon will tell you. Eat for your Moon sign when you need a little extra nourishment and TLC. Don't know your Moon sign? No problem: Cancer is ruled by the Moon, so swim on over for a heartwarming Tomato and Pesto Grilled Cheese Panini and Tomato Soup with Fried Pasta Garnish!

*Foods ruled by the Moon: milk, cheese, yogurt,
butter, bread, pasta, and rice (comfort foods!)*

VENUS: PLANET OF LOVE AND BEAUTY

Venus denotes our preferences—what we like and what we don't like. Your Venus
sign tells you what is pleasurable to your senses. Whether your palate favors salty
or sweet can be decided by your Venus placement. So when you are looking for
some extra satisfaction in your life, whip up some Venus-themed dishes according
to your own Venus sign—or simply head over to Venusian-ruled Taurus for decadent
Tiramisu or to Libra for the perfect Chocolate Mousse. This is something you don't
want to miss!

*Foods ruled by Venus: dessert, chocolate,
sugar, honey, fruit, aphrodisiacs,
and fancy ingredients*

MARS: THE PROPELLER

Need to get motivated? Eat what Mars wants. The red planet represents our drive.
Your Mars sign describes what ignites and excites you. So when you're about to
embark on a new adventure (and you'd like to feel more like Rocky), eat according
to your Mars sign for added courage. Don't know your Mars sign? Aries and Scorpio
are ruled by the warrior planet, so go for Pineapple Salmon or Chilaquiles to elevate
your stamina.

*Foods ruled by Mars: garlic, ginger, cayenne,
paprika, and hot peppers*

MERCURY: PLANET OF INTELLECT

It should be noted that the messenger planet, Mercury, travels closely with the Sun.
Mercury either shares the same sign as your Sun or occupies the sign next door.
Nevertheless, eat according to your Mercury sign when you need to be studious, or
hop on over to Gemini and Virgo (our two Mercurial signs), where you'll surely learn a
thing or two! Grab a plate of Cashew Chicken from Gemini's table or go with Virgo's
Spinach and Ricotta Mini Quiches when you need some extra brain fuel on your side.

Foods ruled by Mercury: nuts and seeds

JUPITER: MORE, MORE, MORE!

Jupiter is the planet of expansion. It's true, sometimes Jupiter just wants to fill up on some greasy pommes frites, but other times Jupiter wants to fill up on experiences—we're talking eye-opening encounters that broaden our understanding, or world travel. Our Jupiter tells us about where we find abundance and significant growth in life. Need a good luck charm? Cook what Jupiter wants! Go with your own Jupiter sign or check out jovial Sagittarius's White Bean Artichoke Dip and Pisces's Breakfast Baklava French Toast to bring more joy into your life!

Foods ruled by Jupiter: oils, fats, fruit, and
all-you-can-eat buffets

SATURN: CONCENTRATE

In astrology, Saturn is the taskmaster. So when that deadline is fast approaching, let Saturn help you get it together. Saturn doesn't believe in excess (that's Jupiter for you), but instead values simplicity. Call on Saturn when you need to get serious and focus on what really matters. Consult your own Saturn sign for recipe inspiration, or call on Capricorn for a plate of Roasted Bay Scallops with Swiss Chard and Aquarius for Classic Chicken Parmesan. These Saturn-infused dishes get straight to the point and don't mess around!

Foods ruled by Saturn: vinegar, acids, sours,
preservatives, bitters, fennel,
parsley, cilantro, and basil

RISING SIGN

The planets beyond Saturn do not have food rulership, because they are beyond the visibility of Earth (unless you want to talk about GMOs, hydroponics, and vertical farming), but there is one last point in your chart worth mentioning: Your Ascendant (also known as your "rising sign") is arguably as important as your Sun sign in determining your personality—as well as your physical body! If you know your rising sign, be sure to enjoy those recipes with as much gusto as your Sun sign!

Cook for Today

As we touched on in the modality section, the Sun's current sign tells us about what season we are in. Want to lounge like a lion during the peak of summer? Go with Leo's Spa Cucumber Smoothie to celebrate August's warmth. Want to get more technical? The Moon is the fastest celestial body, changing signs every two and a half days. The sign the Moon currently travels through influences the collective mood and contributes largely to the overall tone of the day. As we often choose meals based on our mood (especially if you are a water sign!), planning your meals according to the Moon sign is something fun to play with. If this technique calls you, get a Moon calendar and hang it on the refrigerator!

Who's Coming to Dinner?

We've all been a guest at someone's table and walked away thinking, "How do they eat like that?" It's all good; everyone has different tastes. However, this never has to be the case at your house. Impress your family members and friends by cooking for *their* sign. You'll get rave reviews, and, more importantly, they will feel beyond satisfied. Inviting your hot Aquarius date over for dinner for the first time? They'll wonder how you knew Linguine with Asparagus, Parmesan, and Cream was their favorite. Trying to impress your Leo mother-in-law? Serve none other than Pistachio-Crusted Halibut. Throwing a party? Go all out and make sure there's a dish for every sign.

Now that we're star struck and starving, let's get cooking!

Aries:
The Spontaneous Chef

As the first sign of the zodiac, springing forth with the fresh life of spring, you are as straightforward and saucy as they come. Ruled by the passionate warrior planet, Mars, you never hold back your true feelings and desires. Patience is not your thing (neither is tact), but you are a genuine gem who always asserts your truth. You mean what you say, Aries, and as the cardinal fire sign, you are a celestial spitfire! Symbolized by the ram, you move headfirst in life. Some call it bravery, others call it impulsiveness, but either way you slice it, you fearlessly dart where many others fear to tread!

"Act first, think later" is your signature style, which makes life in the kitchen especially interesting. Accidentally added too much cayenne to your soup? Now it's a detox soup. Skipped ahead too far in the recipe and forgot to separate the eggs? You're happy to go with it and see where it leads. You are adventurous, and culinary discoveries are your cup of tea!

Physical activity is of utmost importance for you, Aries, and is sure to get your appetite roaring! As a fire sign who is prone to burnout, you need foods that give you endurance, like the ones in this chapter. You also prefer meals with shorter prep times and love time-saving hacks. So what are you waiting for, Aries? Get those Garlic Knots in the oven!

SWEET POTATO APPLE LATKES

When you start your morning, you need breakfast. And fast! Grating your potatoes takes time and muscle, so cut the prep time in half by quickly grating your potatoes, apple, and onion in your food processor. Sweet potatoes are an ideal food for high-speed Aries due to their earthy, grounding nature (slow it down a notch, Aries!). These toasty griddle cakes are infused with mellow warming spices to complement your fiery nature. Balance that lovable heat with a cooling scoop of applesauce, sour cream, or Greek yogurt for a stellar breakfast that takes no time to whip up!

YIELDS 12 LATKES

3 large sweet potatoes, grated
1 medium apple, cored and grated
1 small yellow onion, peeled and grated
Egg replacer for 2 large eggs
3 tablespoons all-purpose flour

1 teaspoon baking powder
½ teaspoon ground cinnamon
½ teaspoon ground nutmeg
½ teaspoon salt
Canola oil, for frying

1. Using a cloth or paper towel, gently squeeze out excess moisture from potatoes and apples and combine with onion in a large bowl.
2. Add the remaining ingredients except for oil and mix well.
3. Heat ½" oil in a medium skillet over medium-high heat. When the oil is hot, drop the potato mixture in oil ¼ cup at a time and use a spatula to flatten, forming a pancake. Cook 3–4 minutes on each side until lightly crisped. Serve.

CHIVE SCRAMBLE

A quick and easy breakfast that every Aries will appreciate is an egg scramble, and chives are the perfect addition to elevate this dish. Primarily herbal in nature, chives add just enough of a garlicky kick to keep up with you before you head out to the gym, active Aries. Have a Capricorn in the house? Pair this dish with their Homemade Breakfast Sausage Patties (see recipe in the Capricorn chapter) and your favorite whole-grain toast for a balanced breakfast fit for a warrior like you!

SERVES 2

4 large eggs, beaten
½ cup chopped fresh chives
1 tablespoon milk

¼ teaspoon sea salt
¼ teaspoon ground white pepper
1 tablespoon unsalted butter

1. In a medium bowl, whisk together eggs, chives, milk, salt, and pepper.
2. Meanwhile, melt butter in a large skillet over medium heat. Pour the egg mixture into the skillet and use a spatula to move the mixture around, forming curds. Continue to cook, stirring frequently, until eggs are fully cooked, about 3–8 minutes.
3. Divide into two portions and serve immediately.

○ ○ ○ ○ COOL IT ON THE SALT ○ ○ ○ ○

This is probably not the first time someone's told you to "cool it," Aries. Notoriously hotheaded at times, you're also prone to headaches, and dehydration is often to blame. While salt is a prime electrolyte you need to retain water, have too much of it and you'll dry up! Use just the required amount of salt here and fight the urge to add extra before serving.

HONEYDEW ALMOND SMOOTHIE

Three ingredients combine to make the perfect smoothie to cool you down on a hot day (or anytime, really). You're the ignition of the zodiac, energetic Aries, and when your pedal is to the metal, you need a reliable engine coolant—like this green-hued icy treat. Packed with electrolytes, honeydew melon makes this smoothie the perfect frozen treat to keep you level as you cruise through your day. Did we mention that your ruling planet, Mars, also rules engines? So rev up that blender and give it a whirl!

YIELDS 1½ CUPS

2 cups chunked honeydew melon
1 cup almond milk

1 cup ice

1. Combine all the ingredients in a blender and purée until smooth.
2. Serve immediately.

○ ○ ○ ○ SLICE IT UP! ○ ○ ○ ○

Don't even bother trying to wrap up half a melon and store it soundly in the refrigerator. Set yourself up for success by slicing up a couple melons at a time and storing your slices in airtight containers stacked in the freezer—perfect for blending a smoothie in no time while you're flying out the door.

BLACK BEAN AND AVOCADO BURRITOS

Aries really knows how to bring the spice into life—even when hunger strikes! This spicy and simple dish hits all the right notes for spontaneous Aries—it's quick, it's spicy, and there's lots of room for improvising. Want a heartier burrito? Add your favorite protein. Raw onions not your thing? Heat them up in a skillet. Want to ramp up the spice? Add pickled jalapeños and hot sauce. You're in charge of the details, Aries; just try not to inhale these burritos too fast!

SERVES 4

- 4 flour tortillas
- 1 cup canned black beans, drained
- 1½ cups cooked brown rice
- 1 small onion, peeled and chopped into ¼" pieces
- ¼ cup canned or frozen whole-kernel corn, drained
- 2 tablespoons chopped fresh cilantro leaves
- ½ cup shredded lettuce
- ¼ cup canned green chilies
- ¼ teaspoon salt
- ½ teaspoon ground black pepper
- 1 medium avocado, peeled, pitted, and chopped into ½" pieces
- ½ cup shredded Monterey jack cheese
- ¼ cup salsa

1. Preheat oven to 350°F. Place tortillas in a covered container in oven for 5–10 minutes.
2. In a medium bowl, combine beans, rice, onion, corn, cilantro, lettuce, green chilies, salt, and pepper. Mix well.
3. Remove tortillas from oven and place ½ cup bean mixture in the center of each tortilla. Top each with ¼ avocado, 2 tablespoons cheese, and 1 tablespoon salsa.
4. Roll up each tortilla. Fold over the ends before serving.

SALAMI, MOZZARELLA, AND RED ONION PANINI

You love anything that you can eat with your hands, speedy Aries. No silverware means fewer dishes (and more time to play)! A panini is the perfect sandwich to eat hot off the press at home, or even on the go, for active Aries. Bursts of cherry tomato brighten up this sandwich—perfect for someone like you who always brings an energizing spark to the room. Don't have a panini press? No problem! A cast-iron skillet or a filled tea kettle with foil underneath will suffice. Sub out the ciabatta roll for a multigrain one if you've got a long day ahead and need to keep that digestion on a slow burn.

SERVES 1

4 slices salami
1 medium ciabatta roll
¼ cup shredded mozzarella
4 medium cherry tomatoes, halved
¼ medium red onion, peeled and thinly sliced

1 tablespoon olive oil
⅛ teaspoon salt
⅛ teaspoon ground black pepper
1 tablespoon julienned fresh basil leaves

1. Place salami on the bottom half of ciabatta roll. Pile mozzarella and tomatoes on top of salami. Add red onion.
2. Drizzle the sandwich with olive oil. Add salt and pepper and scatter basil leaves. Close the sandwich with the top of roll.
3. Place sandwich on a preheated panini press, close the lid, and cook 3–5 minutes. Remove from the press, slice in half, and serve warm.

GUACAMOLE

Sometimes hunger strikes suddenly, spontaneous Aries, and all you need is a bag of chips and a class-act dip. Guacamole is the answer. Fast and easy to whip up, and incredibly fresh, this slightly spicy and ultra-creamy dip is an all-time favorite. Fresh jalapeños can easily replace the canned, or if you're going for a milder dip, poblanos would be the perfect stand-in. The amount of heat is totally up to you, fiery Aries. Enjoy with your favorite tortilla chips, or, if you have any Guacamole left, pair with Black Bean and Avocado Burritos or Chicken Tortilla Soup (see recipes in this chapter)!

SERVES 8

2 large ripe avocados, peeled, pitted, and cut into 1" pieces

1 medium red tomato, cored and cut into ½" pieces

1 small yellow onion, peeled and cut into ¼" pieces

½ cup canned jalapeños, drained and cut into ¼" pieces

1 tablespoon lime juice

1 teaspoon salt

½ teaspoon ground black pepper

Lime wedges, for garnish

1. In a medium bowl, mash avocados with a fork.
2. Add the remaining ingredients and mix well. Garnish with lime wedges.

○ ○ ○ ○ PIT STOP ○ ○ ○ ○

This recipe makes enough Guacamole to last you a few enjoyable dipping sessions or for a big bowl to share with family or friends. But unfortunately, avocados tend to brown if you don't eat them right away, giving your Guacamole an unappetizing look. Lime juice naturally preserves the Guacamole's green color, but you can keep your Guacamole even brighter and fresher by saving the avocado pits and storing them with your leftover Guacamole.

CUMIN-ROASTED BUTTERNUT SQUASH

Gently browned on the outside and soft on the inside, these melt-in-your-mouth butternut squash cubes will absolutely appeal to your warm Aries nature. Your spontaneous side will delight in mixing this recipe up! Try swapping cumin out for cinnamon and drizzling with maple syrup for a seriously decadent treat. You're game, playful Aries. You'll try anything once. These bite-sized cubes are perfect as an appetizer or even a sneaky late-night snack.

SERVES 8

- 1 (2–3 pound) medium butternut squash
- 2 tablespoons ground cumin
- 2 tablespoons olive oil
- ⅛ teaspoon salt
- ⅛ teaspoon coarsely ground black pepper
- 1 tablespoon roughly chopped fresh Italian (flat-leaf) parsley

1. Preheat oven to 375°F.
2. Cut squash in two just above the bulbous bottom. Place the cut side of the top part down on a cutting board and peel it with a knife or potato peeler, removing all rind. Repeat with the bottom part, then cut bottom in half and remove seeds. Dice squash into 1" chunks.
3. In a large mixing bowl, toss squash with cumin, oil, salt, and pepper.
4. Spread in a single layer on a baking sheet and roast in oven 40 minutes, turning after 25 minutes, until browned and tender.
5. Serve sprinkled with parsley.

GARLIC KNOTS

Like you, sharpshooting Aries, garlic packs a serious punch!
Especially when baked into soft homemade rolls. Bold Aries is unafraid
of taking risks, so you might feel tempted to push the limits and
add even more garlic. Go for it!

SERVES 4

3½ teaspoons olive oil, divided
1 (0.25-ounce) packet dry active yeast
2½ cups warm water (should not exceed 115°F)
5 cups whole-wheat flour
2 cups all-purpose flour

⅛ teaspoon salt
1 cup room temperature water
1 bulb garlic, peeled and minced
½ teaspoon ground black pepper
1 teaspoon dried parsley
¼ cup freshly grated Parmesan cheese

1. Lightly grease a 13" × 9" baking pan with 1 teaspoon olive oil.
2. In a small bowl, stir together yeast and warm water and let stand about 5 minutes until foamy.
3. In a large bowl, sift together flours and salt.
4. Mix together the flour mixture, dissolved yeast mixture, and water by hand or in a mixer with a dough hook until the dough forms a ball. Remove from the mixing bowl, place in a clean bowl, and cover with a clean kitchen towel. Let rise in a warm place for about 45 minutes.
5. Knead the dough for 3 minutes, place in prepared pan, and cover with a towel. Let rise again for about 30 minutes.
6. Lightly grease a baking sheet with 1½ teaspoons olive oil.
7. Roll out the dough on a floured surface to 1" thickness and cut into four 12" strands. Tie each strip loosely into a knot, stretching gently if necessary to make 4" knots. Place the knots on prepared baking sheet, cover with a clean kitchen towel, and let rise in a warm place.
8. Preheat oven to 425°F.
9. Sprinkle the dough knots with remaining 1 teaspoon olive oil, then sprinkle with garlic, pepper, and parsley.
10. Bake 15–20 minutes. Sprinkle with cheese and serve.

CHICKEN TORTILLA SOUP

*This recipe is ideal for Aries's short attention spans. Just chop and prep all
the ingredients, toss in a stockpot, and let the stove work its magic. Easy!
The only hard part for you, impatient Aries, is the waiting, but you know that
a soup this tasty is well worth the wait. Your competitive nature will also love
when your guests sing your praises over your culinary conquests, so serve
this one up with some tortilla chips and feel victorious!*

SERVES 8

- 1 whole rotisserie chicken with skin removed, cut into 1" pieces
- 1 medium white onion, peeled and chopped into ¼" pieces
- 4 cloves garlic, minced
- 1 medium red bell pepper, seeded and chopped into ¼" pieces
- 3 medium red tomatoes, cored and chopped into 1" pieces
- 2 (15-ounce) cans black beans, drained

- 2 tablespoons chili powder
- 2 teaspoons salt
- 1 tablespoon ground cumin
- ½ teaspoon red pepper flakes
- 1 teaspoon granulated sugar
- 2 cups canned or frozen corn, drained
- 6 cups chicken broth
- ¼ cup lime juice
- 4 tostadas
- 1 bunch fresh cilantro, stems removed

1. In a large stockpot, combine all the ingredients except lime juice, tostadas, and cilantro. Bring to a boil and cook 20 minutes. Reduce heat to low, cover, and simmer 2 hours. Stir in lime juice right before serving.
2. Break tostadas into small pieces. Sprinkle tostada pieces and cilantro leaves on the soup before serving.

ASPARAGUS SALAD WITH HARD-BOILED EGGS

Aries are usually built with strong bodies and strong immune systems. You need a salad as tough as you are. The hard-boiled eggs in this salad offer plenty of protein to help sporty Aries between workouts, while asparagus is a powerful ally of the immune system with anti-inflammatory properties and antioxidants. Cooling dill and fresh parsley add a delicious herbal layer to this salad that will leave you wishing you'd made more! Eggs can be boiled in advance and stored in the refrigerator until you are ready to nosh.

SERVES 4

1½ pounds steamed asparagus, bottoms trimmed
2 large hard-boiled eggs, coarsely grated
3 tablespoons white wine vinegar
3 tablespoons olive oil
½ teaspoon Dijon mustard
2 tablespoons lemon juice
½ tablespoon lemon zest
2 tablespoons minced fresh dill
1 tablespoon minced fresh Italian parsley
¼ teaspoon sea salt

1. In a large bowl, toss together asparagus and eggs. Set aside.
2. In a small bowl, whisk together vinegar, oil, mustard, lemon juice, lemon zest, dill, parsley, and salt. Drizzle over asparagus and egg. Toss lightly. Serve immediately.

RATATOUILLE

There are no rules to this fresh, fragrant French vegetable medley.
So let spontaneity be your muse as you peruse the produce aisle. That
said, the vegetables included in this versatile recipe are right up your alley.
Gourds are the perfect balancing act to your fiery constitution, offering you
grounding and nourishment with their softer properties, while the olives will
quench your thirst for salt. Pair this bright, aromatic feast of vegetables with
toasty Garlic Knots (see recipe in this chapter) and your favorite protein
to make this a meal that's beyond complete.

SERVES 6

½ teaspoon olive oil

1 small eggplant, trimmed and chopped

1 small zucchini, trimmed and chopped

1 small yellow squash, trimmed and chopped

½ medium leek, trimmed and chopped

1 medium shallot, peeled and minced

2 cloves garlic, minced

1 medium plum tomato, cored and diced

1 tablespoon chopped fresh thyme

1 cup vegetable broth

¼ cup chopped kalamata olives

1 teaspoon ground black pepper

1. Heat oil in a large saucepan or Dutch oven over medium-high heat. Sauté eggplant, zucchini, squash, leek, shallot, and garlic until slightly softened, about 8 minutes.
2. Add tomato, thyme, and broth. Bring to a boil, then reduce heat to low. Cover and simmer 20 minutes.
3. Add olives and pepper; cook another 5 minutes. Serve hot or at room temperature.

PINEAPPLE SALMON

Aries, you can sometimes get a little hotheaded, so here's a meal to help you stay even-keeled. Both pineapple and salmon are anti-inflammatory, which can help prevent those headaches and sinus issues that so often trip you up. Also, pineapple is an excellent digestive aid (you know, in case you eat too fast). In the body, Aries rules the head. Packed with nutritious fats that nourish the eyes and brain, salmon is an ideal protein for you, Aries. After a long day of slaying, serve this dish over a bed of wild rice and pair with your favorite pilsner to cap off the day.

SERVES 4

1 medium pineapple, peeled, cored, and cut into ¼" rings
4 (5-ounce) salmon fillets
¼ cup soy sauce
2 teaspoons sesame oil
2 teaspoons toasted sesame seeds
1 bunch scallions, chopped (ends trimmed)

1. Preheat oven to 350°F.
2. Tear off four 2' lengths of foil. Evenly divide the pineapple among the foil. Place one salmon fillet on top of the pineapple in each packet.
3. In a small bowl, whisk together soy sauce, sesame oil, sesame seeds, and scallions. Spoon an even amount of sauce over each fillet. Fold the foil packets shut.
4. Bake 30 minutes or until salmon is fully cooked. Serve.

OVEN-BAKED CHICKEN WINGS

These wings have the spice that Aries adores, but the Homemade Peach Barbecue Sauce adds an irresistible sweet, sticky dimension to your wings that will have you shamelessly licking your fingers clean. These wings will go quick, so double the recipe if necessary.

--- **SERVES 6** ---

WINGS

5 pounds chicken wings
1½ tablespoons hot paprika
1½ tablespoons chili powder
2 tablespoons ground mustard powder
1 teaspoon ground cayenne
1 teaspoon crushed chipotle pepper
 flakes
1 teaspoon garlic powder
1 teaspoon sea salt
1 teaspoon ground black pepper

HOMEMADE PEACH BARBECUE SAUCE

1 medium shallot, peeled and chopped
1¾ pounds peaches, peeled and halved
2 tablespoons water
¼ cup Worcestershire sauce
½ cup apple cider vinegar
2 tablespoons mustard powder
½ teaspoon cayenne pepper
1 tablespoon unsalted butter
½ teaspoon hickory liquid smoke
 (optional)

1. Preheat oven to 300°F.
2. Place wings and spices in a large resealable plastic bag. Shake to coat.
3. Arrange wings on broiling pans or wire rack–lined baking sheets. Bake 25 minutes.
4. Raise the temperature to 450°F. Bake 30–40 minutes or until wings are crisp and golden.
5. While wings are cooking, make the sauce: Pulse all the sauce ingredients in a blender until smooth.
6. Pour into a small saucepan and simmer on low 15 minutes or until heated through and slightly thickened.
7. Drain wings on paper towel–lined plates if needed. Then place wings in a large bowl. Drizzle with about 1 cup sauce and toss to coat. Serve immediately.

CHILES RELLENOS EN CROÛTE WITH TOMATO AND CILANTRO SAUCE

Energetic Aries love hosting dinner parties. They aim to create a fun and memorable atmosphere for their guests. Chiles rellenos is the perfect dish for a charming Aries to show off some presentation skills.

SERVES 4

---

4 fresh poblano peppers
¾ pound Monterey jack cheese, grated
½ pound goat cheese, crumbled
2 sticks butter
4 sheets whole-wheat phyllo dough
1 large yellow onion, peeled and cut
   into ¼" pieces

1 tablespoon olive oil
16 Roma tomatoes, cored and cut into
   ¼" pieces
1 teaspoon salt
4 bunches fresh cilantro, stems
   removed and leaves chopped in
   ¼" pieces

---

1. Preheat oven to 350°F.
2. Put peppers on a baking sheet and roast about 20 minutes or until well browned. (Leave oven at 350°F.) Remove peppers from oven and place in a paper bag; close tightly and let peppers cool. Remove the skin, stems, and seeds when cool. Do not cut peppers open other than at the top.
3. In a medium bowl, combine the cheeses.
4. Fill each pepper with ¼ cheese mixture.
5. In a small saucepan over low heat, melt butter. Lay phyllo sheets out flat on a work surface. Take one sheet of phyllo at a time and brush with butter, using a pastry brush. Put one chili in the corner of one sheet of phyllo and roll up, brushing all unbuttered surfaces with butter. Repeat with remaining peppers.
6. Place the chiles rellenos on a baking sheet and bake 20–25 minutes or until phyllo is well browned.
7. In a medium saucepan over medium heat, sauté onion in olive oil until onion is clear and limp. Add tomatoes and cook 5–10 minutes or until liquid has evaporated. Add salt and cilantro. Stir well.
8. To serve, pour the sauce on a plate and top with chiles rellenos.

GINGER CREAMS

*Spunky Aries love a gingery zing! So you absolutely cannot go wrong
with Ginger Creams—sweet ginger cookies sandwiching irresistible
cream cheese icing. These cookies are made with high-fiber flaxseed and
molasses, which offer robust flavors that pair perfectly with ginger and also
lend these cookies a divine chewiness. Want to achieve fluffier frosting?
Then try incorporating whipped cream cheese. Not big on frosting? Choose
a smoother cream cheese and give a light schmear to each cookie.*

YIELDS 24 COOKIES

COOKIES

⅓ cup butter, softened
½ cup brown sugar
1 large egg
¼ cup molasses
¼ cup honey
½ cup orange juice
1 teaspoon vanilla extract
1 cup whole-wheat pastry flour
1 cup all-purpose flour
¼ cup wheat germ
2 tablespoons ground flaxseed
2 teaspoons ground ginger

½ teaspoon ground cinnamon
¼ teaspoon salt
1 teaspoon baking soda

FROSTING

2 tablespoons butter, softened
3 (3-ounce) packages cream cheese,
  softened
⅓ cup sour cream
4 cups confectioners' sugar, divided,
  plus more for dusting
2 teaspoons vanilla extract
⅛ teaspoon salt

1. Preheat oven to 375°F.
2. In a large bowl, combine butter, brown sugar, and egg and beat until fluffy. Add
   molasses, honey, orange juice, and vanilla and beat until smooth.
3. In a medium bowl, combine flours, wheat germ, flaxseed, ginger, cinnamon,
   salt, and baking soda and mix well. Add to the butter mixture and stir until a
   batter forms.
4. Drop the batter by teaspoons onto ungreased cookie sheets. Bake 9–12 minutes or until the cookies are set and light golden brown. Cool on sheet
   4 minutes, then remove to wire racks to cool completely.
5. While the cookies cool, make the frosting: In a large bowl, combine butter,
   cream cheese, and sour cream; beat well until fluffy.

6. Add half the confectioners' sugar; beat until fluffy. Stir in vanilla and salt and beat well. Add remaining confectioners' sugar, beating constantly until frosting reaches desired spreading consistency.

7. Once cookies are cool, spread about 1 tablespoon frosting on the bottom of one cookie and top with a second cookie, bottom-side down, and press together gently to form a "sandwich." Repeat with remaining cookies. Sprinkle with extra confectioners' sugar and serve.

ROCKY ROAD BROWNIES

Ardent Aries, all you ever really need in life is chocolate. That's why you're getting this recipe for ooey-gooey marshmallows melted over rich chocolate fudge brownies. Aries love rocky road ice cream, so you're guaranteed to go nuts for these fluffy, chocolaty Rocky Road Brownies. Speaking of nuts, these brownies are topped with toasted hazelnuts, adding a seriously satisfying crunch. These Rocky Road Brownies are out-of-this-world delicious and ideal for bold Aries after a satisfying meal or after hitting the batting cages.

SERVES 24

½ cup water
⅓ cup butter
1 cup cocoa powder
1 cup granulated sugar
¾ cup brown sugar
½ cup low-fat sour cream
1 cup all-purpose flour
1 cup whole-wheat pastry flour
1 teaspoon baking powder

½ teaspoon baking soda
¼ teaspoon salt
2 teaspoons vanilla extract
2 large eggs
4 large egg whites
1 cup mini marshmallows
½ cup chopped toasted hazelnuts
½ cup dark chocolate chips

1. Preheat oven to 325°F. Grease an 8" × 8" pan with nonstick cooking spray or butter.
2. In a large microwave-safe bowl, combine water, butter, and cocoa powder. Microwave on high 1 minute, then remove and stir. Continue microwaving on high for 30-second intervals until the mixture boils.
3. Remove from the microwave and add sugars; mix well. Add sour cream, flours, baking powder, baking soda, salt, and vanilla and mix until combined.
4. Stir in eggs and egg whites until blended. Pour into prepared pan. Bake 22–26 minutes or until brownies are set. A toothpick inserted in the center should come out clean.
5. Immediately sprinkle with marshmallows; return to oven. Bake 3–4 minutes longer until marshmallows puff. Remove from oven and sprinkle with hazelnuts and dark chocolate chips. Cool on wire rack, then cut into squares.

TEQUILA SUNRISE MARGARITA

Spontaneous Aries can look forward to combining their two favorite tequila drinks into one sunny-hued beverage. This single sipper combines the best of both worlds—the orangey hue of a tequila sunrise and the distinctive tang of a margarita. You and your guests will get a kick out of this thirst-quenching summery fusion. This is the drink you need to cool down and turn up at the same time.

SERVES 1

Kosher salt, for rimming
1½ ounces blanco tequila
½ ounce grenadine
½ ounce triple sec

1 ounce sweet and sour mix
1 ounce orange juice
1 cup ice
1 lime wheel

1. Rim a margarita glass with salt.
2. Pour the liquid ingredients into a blender along with ice and blend until smooth.
3. Pour into the glass and garnish with lime wheel.

Taurus:
The Smooth Chef

Sensual Tauruses swoon from the luxurious experiences of the five senses. As an earth sign ruled by Venus, goddess of beauty, money, and pleasure, this indulgent bull has fine taste. A fancy night out to a five-star restaurant or a pedicure can be a most intoxicating experience for these cosmic bulls! Looking to win a Taurus over? Try an expensive candle, silky sheets, and handmade designer chocolates. Fancy Taureans can look forward to a breakfast as pleasing to the eyes as it is to the palate with the pink-hued Raspberry Waffles in this chapter.

As a Taurus, you prefer to take your time, moving at your own pace. If someone prods you, you will dig your heels in! Yes, Taurus is a fixed sign and can be quite stubborn! But you are as consistent and loyal as they come. For cautious Venusian folks like you, love is earned. You have integrity and simply cannot be bothered wasting your time with anything flimsy. Beauteous Taurus delights in preparing decadent dishes with the finest ingredients; plating and stunning presentation come naturally to you. Taurus brings a smooth elegance to the table, favoring recipes that are simple, solid, and decadent. There's something about a buildup that makes the food all the tastier, which is why you don't mind waiting for a dish like Potatoes Au Gratin Casserole. Leave it to the gourmet of the zodiac to tantalize the senses with a full-bodied culinary experience.

MEDITERRANEAN OMELET

As a sensual earth sign, texture is high on the priority list for you, and in this recipe egg whites and yogurt combine to deliver an unrivaled fluffy texture that's sure to excite the senses. Taurus tends to like the flavor of bacon, and luckily, pancetta has a starring role in this recipe. Pancetta is like bacon, but without the smoky flavor. It's sweet, salty, fatty, and decadent in all the right ways. Your taste buds are guaranteed to swoon from this quality omelet, so warm up the pan and settle in.

SERVES 6

2 large eggs
6 large egg whites
¼ cup plain nonfat yogurt
2 teaspoons olive oil, divided

2 ounces pancetta, sliced paper-thin
3 ounces Swiss cheese, shredded
¼ cup chopped fresh parsley
½ teaspoon ground black pepper

1. In a medium bowl, beat eggs and egg whites, then whisk in yogurt.
2. Heat 1 teaspoon oil in a small skillet over medium-high heat. Quickly sauté pancetta until crisp, about 2 minutes, then remove and drain on a paper towel.
3. Heat remaining oil in a large sauté pan over medium heat. Pour in the egg mixture, then sprinkle in pancetta and cheese. Stir once only. Continuously move the pan, using a spatula to push the egg edge inward slightly to allow the egg mixture to pour outward and solidify. Cook until mostly firm, about 5 minutes, then use a spatula to fold egg mixture in half.
4. Reduce heat to low, cover, and cook approximately 3 minutes more. Sprinkle with parsley and pepper and serve.

RASPBERRY WAFFLES

Beauteous Taurus simply cannot resist a pink pastry. And that's just one reason these cosmic bulls are guaranteed to adore Raspberry Waffles. The other reason? Waffles. Indulgent Tauruses love pastries at any time of the day, but especially at breakfast. You often won't even bother cooking unless you're going all out, Taurus, so lay that maple syrup on thick. One last tip? These waffles are best enjoyed while wearing your silk robe and fuzzy slippers, posh Taurus!

SERVES 4

1 cup all-purpose flour
1 cup white whole-wheat flour
1 tablespoon light brown sugar
1 tablespoon baking powder
¼ teaspoon kosher salt
1 teaspoon vanilla extract
2 tablespoons canola oil

1 large egg, room temperature
1 cup buttermilk, room temperature
1 cup sour cream, room temperature
1 cup fresh raspberries, plus more for garnish
Confectioners' sugar, for dusting

1. In a large bowl, whisk together flours, brown sugar, baking powder, and salt.
2. In a small bowl, whisk together vanilla, oil, egg, buttermilk, and sour cream until smooth. Pour into the dry ingredients and stir to combine. Fold in raspberries.
3. Cook in a Belgian-style waffle maker according to manufacturer's instructions. Serve immediately, garnished with fresh raspberries and a dusting of confectioners' sugar or keep warm in a 200°F oven.

LOBSTER RAVIOLI

Lobster Ravioli is an indulgent dish designed for gourmet Taureans everywhere. Posh Taurus loves everything about lobster—it's decadent, buttery, and fancy—especially when it is enveloped in homemade garlic pasta and served up with a creamy mascarpone cheese sauce. Pasta dough can be made an hour (or up to a day) ahead. Aim for a thicker dough, because the ravioli needs to be able to hold the buttery lobster filling as it boils. The end result? A meal supremely rich in flavor and guaranteed to satisfy classy Taureans when hunger calls!

SERVES 10

ROASTED GARLIC PASTA

1 cup durum wheat (semolina) flour
1 cup whole-wheat flour
2 cups all-purpose flour
⅛ teaspoon iodized salt
2 large eggs
¼ cup extra-virgin olive oil
¼ cup water
2 cloves garlic
3 tablespoons olive oil, divided

FILLING

2 pounds fresh uncooked lobster meat, chopped into bite-sized pieces

2 bunches leeks, trimmed and thinly sliced
½ bunch fresh parsley, chopped
½ teaspoon ground black pepper

MASCARPONE CHEESE SAUCE

½ cup unsalted butter
½ cup all-purpose flour
4 cups whole milk
2 cups light cream
½ pound mascarpone cheese

1. In a large bowl, sift together flours and salt.
2. In a small bowl, whisk eggs. Whisk in extra-virgin olive oil and water.
3. Make a well in the center of the flour and pour in the egg mixture. Mix together the wet and dry ingredients by hand or in a mixer with a dough hook until fully incorporated and the dough forms a ball. Wrap the dough in plastic wrap and let it rest in the refrigerator at least 1 hour or up to 1 day. Allow the dough to return to room temperature if it has rested in the refrigerator for more than 1 hour.

4. Mash garlic and 2 tablespoons olive oil together with a mortar and pestle until it forms a paste. Set aside.
5. Separate the dough into two balls. Roll out one ball on a floured surface into a sheet about ¼" thick. Brush very lightly with remaining 1 tablespoon olive oil and spread garlic paste on the dough. Roll out the other ball into a sheet the same size as the first and place it on top of the first sheet of dough. Roll to ensure that the sheets are stuck together.
6. Roll out the pasta dough on a floured surface into sheets about ½" thick. Cut into circles 3" in diameter.
7. In a large bowl, mix together lobster, leeks, parsley, and black pepper.
8. Spoon teaspoonfuls of the lobster mixture onto the centers of the circles. Lightly paint the outer edges of the pasta circles with a tiny amount of water, fold the circles in half, and seal by pressing closed with your fingers.
9. Fill a large pot ¾ full with water and bring to a slow boil. Add the ravioli and cook until al dente, approximately 10 minutes.
10. While the ravioli cooks, make the cheese sauce: Melt butter in a large saucepan over medium heat. Sprinkle in flour and stir with a wooden spoon. Whisk in milk and cream (be careful not to scorch the sauce). Simmer until the sauce thickens, about 10 minutes. Remove from heat and stir in cheese.
11. Drain ravioli and serve with the cheese sauce.

∘ ∘ ∘ ∘ **ODE TO MASCARPONE** ∘ ∘ ∘ ∘

Mascarpone sounds fancy, but it is very simple. Mascarpone is like an unsweetened cream cheese or an ultra-silky butter. It doesn't have much flavor on its own, leaving its creaminess as the major contribution to any dish or dessert. Exhibit A: this smooth, easy-to-make cheese sauce. Enjoy, decadent Taurus.

FIG, PROSCIUTTO, AND BRIE BRUSCHETTA

Finally—a bruschetta up to luxurious Taurus's standards. This slightly indulgent bruschetta features savory prosciutto and is complemented by the slightly sweet addition of fresh figs. Depending on where you live, figs can be a seasonal delicacy—just the thing to make plush Taurus feel ultra-fancy. If figs are unavailable, opt for a fig spread to sweeten this snack even further. Warm, soft, and unbelievably delicious, Brie is the ultimate Taurean cheese. Not indulgent enough for you yet, dear Taurus? Push the pleasure limit by dotting the bruschetta with morsels of dark chocolate. Heaven on earth!

SERVES 6

6 thin slices Italian bread
2 tablespoons olive oil
12 ounces Brie, sliced into 12 slices
6 thin slices prosciutto

3 medium fresh figs, sliced
⅛ teaspoon salt
⅛ teaspoon ground black pepper

1. Preheat broiler. Brush both sides of bread with olive oil and place on a baking sheet. Broil slices until lightly toasted, about 2 minutes per side.
2. Top each bread slice with two slices Brie, one slice prosciutto, and 2–3 fig slices. Sprinkle with salt and pepper and serve immediately.

○ ○ ○ ○ RUFFLES AND FRILLS ○ ○ ○ ○

It's true: You have fine taste, Taurus, and once you discover the top-shelf item that is perfect in every way, you'll boast its superiority. And since you're the gourmet of the zodiac, we'll take your word for it. Whether for a fancy dinner party you're hosting or for just hanging at home, you have a love of premium items, so you want all the ruffles and frills even if it's a jar of imported fig spread that's $13.

GREEN ENERGY SMOOTHIE

As a classy Taurus, you adore anything that makes you feel like you're living your best life—like this smoothie. Made with spinach, but also with generous servings of fresh fruit, this Green Energy Smoothie will appeal to sweet-toothed Taureans, who can take comfort that this healthy afternoon sipper is still plenty sweet. Yes, Taurus's love of sugar is real—and all the more reason to hit those protein and mineral benchmarks during the day to keep those cravings in check. Spinach assists in hitting your iron count, while protein-rich yogurt lends a creaminess that all sensual bulls will adore.

YIELDS 1½ CUPS

½ cup baby spinach
1 medium apple, cored
1 medium banana, peeled
1 cup low-fat plain yogurt

6 medium strawberries, stems removed
½ medium orange, peeled

1. Place all the ingredients in a blender and process until smooth.
2. Serve immediately.

○ ○ ○ ○ SO COMFORTABLE ○ ○ ○ ○

It's true what they say about you, plush Taurus: You like to be comfy. Lazy at times, you are highly selective about which endeavors are worth your energy. If you want something bad enough, you'll work up the momentum and become unstoppable! This smoothie's here to help!

GRILLED BROCCOLI RABE AND ALFREDO RISOTTO

Tauruses are enamored by a dish that is both beautiful and sumptuous, and this one checks all the boxes. Buttery, cheesy, and slightly sinful, Alfredo sauce is an ingredient highly revered by gourmet Taurus—and especially so when it's homemade! This recipe uses fontina cheese, butter, and white wine, and is guaranteed to seduce indulgent Tauruses into a culinary love spell. Risotto is one of the plushest grains around, which means it can absorb more of that divinely creamy Alfredo sauce. You always look forward to lunch, dear Taurus, but this one in particular!

SERVES 10

2 pounds broccoli rabe
5 tablespoons olive oil, divided
¼ teaspoon ground black pepper
2 medium shallots, peeled and minced
2 cloves garlic, minced
2½ cups arborio rice

½ cup dry white wine (not cooking wine)
6 cups stock of choice
1½ cups cream
¼ cup cold unsalted butter
¼ cup shredded fontina cheese

1. Preheat the grill. In a medium bowl, toss broccoli rabe in 4 tablespoons oil and sprinkle with pepper. Grill 2 minutes on each side.
2. Heat remaining oil over medium heat in a large saucepan. Sauté shallots and garlic 5 minutes. Add rice and stir 2 minutes.
3. Add wine and stir until completely absorbed. Add stock ½ cup at a time, stirring frequently and allowing each addition to be completely absorbed before adding the next. Continue until all stock is absorbed and rice is tender.
4. In a small saucepan over medium-high heat, heat cream until reduced by half the volume, about 15–20 minutes. Add butter a bit at a time and stir to incorporate before adding more. Remove from heat and stir in cheese.
5. To serve, mound rice in serving bowls, top with broccoli rabe, and drizzle with Alfredo sauce.

NOT-SO-SINFUL POTATO SKINS

Not everything needs to be dripping in butter to fulfill your sometimes-hedonistic desires. Sometimes, your wish is to keep things plain and simple. You're a practical earth sign, after all. Feel free to use whatever cheese you have on hand or use plain Greek yogurt in place of sour cream. And if you have a hankering for bacon bits, no one's going to stop you, insistent Taurus! For those days when you need a solid standby to lean on, this one's for you, Taurus.

SERVES 6

6 medium baking potatoes
½ teaspoon salt
⅛ teaspoon ground black pepper
½ cup shredded fat-free Cheddar
  cheese

¼ cup sliced green onions
½ cup fat-free sour cream

1. Preheat oven to 475°F. Coat a large baking sheet with nonstick cooking spray.
2. Cut potatoes in half and scoop out 90 percent of the flesh. Place potato halves on baking sheet and sprinkle with salt and pepper. Bake 10–15 minutes or until crispy.
3. Sprinkle potatoes with cheese and return to oven for 2 minutes. Remove, sprinkle potatoes with onions and serve with a dollop of sour cream.

ROASTED TOMATOES WITH WHITE BEANS AND MARINATED ARTICHOKES

Here's an appetizer that does not skip over a Taurean necessity: rich flavor. Artichokes were used as aphrodisiacs in ancient times to set the mood for love. In fact, the word "aphrodisiac" stems from your planetary ruler's Grecian incarnation, Aphrodite. So for you, Venusian Taurus, artichokes are an exotic ingredient you can routinely relish in. They pair well with the Italian seasonings you adore, they're full of antioxidants, and they lower blood sugar (something every Taurus needs to watch out for). You're big on flavor, Taurus, so you'll be obsessed with the toasty notes the cast-iron skillet adds to this already flavorful dish. Treat yourself!

SERVES 4

- 3 tablespoons olive oil
- 2 pints cherry tomatoes
- 2 tablespoons minced fresh oregano
- 2 tablespoons minced fresh basil
- 1 tablespoon minced fresh Italian parsley
- 1 teaspoon ground black pepper
- ½ teaspoon sea salt
- 8 ounces canned marinated artichokes, drained
- 25 ounces cooked cannellini beans

---

1. Preheat oven to 425°F.
2. In a medium bowl, toss oil and tomatoes together. Pour into a 12" cast-iron skillet. Roast 10–15 minutes or until tomatoes are soft.
3. Place skillet on stovetop and add the remaining ingredients. Sauté over medium heat until beans are heated through, about 5–10 minutes. Serve.

ARUGULA, PEAR, AND GOAT CHEESE SALAD

Most salads do not impress you, Taurus. You tend to gravitate to dishes that are hearty and soulful, which usually does not equate with salad. Fret not, sophisticated foodie, for this salad has everything it takes to meet your refined palate's standards of texture, flavor, and presentation. Creamy goat cheese pairs stupendously with vibrant pistachios for an immaculate crunch, while pears offer you the sweetness you crave, insatiable Taurus. You'll surely feel the love on this one. This salad is satisfying enough on its own, but go ahead and "pear" it with the Smooth Cauliflower Soup with Coriander (see recipe in this chapter).

--- **SERVES 6** ---

- 2 medium pears, cored and cut into wedges
- 2 tablespoons fresh lemon juice, divided
- 1 tablespoon balsamic vinegar
- 1/3 cup extra-virgin olive oil
- 1/4 cup chopped fresh chives
- 1/2 teaspoon salt
- 1/8 teaspoon ground black pepper
- 3 cups arugula
- 1/2 cup chopped unsalted pistachios
- 1/2 cup crumbled goat cheese

1. In a small bowl, toss pears with 1 tablespoon lemon juice.
2. In a large bowl, whisk remaining lemon juice, vinegar, oil, chives, salt, and pepper.
3. Add arugula to a large bowl and toss to coat. Transfer to a serving platter.
4. Arrange pears over arugula and sprinkle with pistachios and cheese.
5. Drizzle any remaining dressing over the salad and serve.

SMOOTH CAULIFLOWER SOUP WITH CORIANDER

Good news for willful bulls everywhere: You can satisfy your cravings for a creamy culinary experience without using actual cream. That's right, Taurus; you can have your cake and eat it too. Cauliflower is your secret weapon, capable of satisfying multiple cravings at a lower-calorie tier, so that you never have to sacrifice your high-end cravings. This recipe calls for milk, but you can easily substitute with a plain nondairy alternative. White wine lends a light acidity to this soup, bringing out the rich herbal flavors appreciated by a flavor savant like you. Enjoy hot out of the saucepan or chilled the following day. And for bonus Taurus points:
Top with crispy bacon! Ooh la la!

SERVES 5

2 tablespoons unsalted butter
1 medium onion, peeled and chopped
2 tablespoons white wine or dry sherry
1 medium head (about 2 pounds) cauliflower, cored and cut into bite-sized pieces

2 cups vegetable stock
1 teaspoon salt
1/8 teaspoon ground white pepper
1 teaspoon ground coriander
3/4 cup cold milk
Chopped chives or parsley, for garnish

1. In a large saucepan or soup pot over medium-high heat, melt butter. Add onion; cook until it is translucent but not brown, about 5 minutes.
2. Add wine and cauliflower; cook 1 minute to steam out the alcohol. Add stock, salt, pepper, and coriander; bring up to a rolling boil.
3. Simmer until cauliflower is very tender, about 15 minutes. Transfer to a blender.
4. Add half the milk and purée until very smooth, scraping down the sides of the blender with a rubber spatula. Be very careful during this step, since hot liquids will splash out of blender if it is not started gradually (you may wish to purée in two batches, for safety).
5. Transfer soup back to saucepan and thin with additional milk if necessary. Garnish with chopped herbs just before serving.

OYSTERS ON THE HALF SHELL WITH MIGNONETTE SAUCE

The stars predict romance in your future with this lovestruck dish! Oysters are the ultimate aphrodisiac, rumored to induce dopamine production, also known as "nature's high." Oysters are best consumed raw, so let your high culinary standards lead you to the freshest oysters available. Exotic, sensual, and fancy, this is one blissful treat you'll love getting your hands on.

SERVES 4

MIGNONETTE SAUCE

- ⅔ cup sparkling rosé wine
- 2 tablespoons red wine vinegar
- ½ teaspoon ground black pepper
- 2 tablespoons finely diced red onions or shallots
- 1 tablespoon finely diced radishes

OYSTERS

- 16 live fresh oysters
- 4 cups crushed ice
- 1 large lemon, cut into wedges

1. Bring wine and vinegar to a boil in a small pot over medium heat. Reduce heat to medium-low, and cook until liquid is reduced by half.
2. Remove pot from heat and add pepper, onions, and radishes.
3. Let sauce cool to room temperature before serving.
4. Place an oyster on a steady work surface with the hinged end facing up. Using a tea towel to help you hold the oyster, grip it with one hand. With the other hand, carefully stick a knife or oyster shucker into the hinge. Dig the knife into the hinge, wiggling the knife until the shell begins to open.
5. Slide the knife across the top shell to disconnect the muscle from the shell.
6. Discard the top shell. Slip the knife underneath the oyster and disconnect it from the bottom shell. Remove any pieces of dirt or broken shell.
7. Repeat this process with remaining oysters.
8. Place oysters (in their bottom shells) on a bed of crushed ice with lemon wedges and prepared sauce on the side.

LINGUINE CARBONARA

Any Taurus will attest that everything is better with bacon. Its distinctively salty flavor adds an indulgently comforting elegance to any dish. So when that craving strikes, you may as well combine it with your other true love: pasta. Popularized in America after WWII, carbonara is rumored to be named for the hardworking miners who needed a tasty and filling meal at the end of the day. You, too, know how to bring home the bacon, Taurus!

SERVES 6

1 tablespoon salt
1 pound linguine pasta
4 large egg yolks
2 teaspoons ground black pepper
1 cup grated Romano cheese, divided
¾ cup diced bacon or pancetta

3 tablespoons water
¼ cup extra-virgin olive oil
¼ cup diced red onions
2 cloves garlic, smashed
¼ cup dry white wine

1. Fill a large pot ⅔ full with water and place it over medium-high heat. Add salt and bring water to a boil. Add pasta and cook 6–7 minutes or until al dente (follow the package's cooking times).
2. In a small bowl, whisk egg yolks, pepper, and 3/4 cup Romano. Set aside.
3. To a large skillet over medium-high heat, add bacon and water. Cook bacon until crispy but not hard. Remove bacon with a slotted spoon and set aside. Discard all but 1 tablespoon bacon fat from the skillet.
4. Add oil to skillet and heat 30 seconds over medium heat. Add onions and garlic and cook 1–2 minutes.
5. Add wine and deglaze the pan for 2 minutes. Remove from heat and stir in reserved bacon.
6. Reserve ¼ cup pasta cooking water and drain pasta. Add pasta, pasta water, and the egg mixture to the skillet. The residual heat of the hot pasta and pasta water should cook and bind the egg mixture into a thick and creamy sauce. Serve topped with remaining cheese.

GOAT CHEESE–STUFFED DATES

For how decadent these bite-sized treats are, they are surprisingly simple to prepare. Whether you're serving four people or fifty, this is a wonderful hors d'oeuvre to offer at your party. Dates are infamously sweet (which your sweet tooth will obviously love), though they are high in minerals and rate surprisingly low on the glycemic index (all good things, Taurus). The thing you'll love most about this recipe, sensual Taurus, is that you'll get to use a special delicacy: culinary lavender. Not all lavender is edible, so do your research before harvesting from the garden.

SERVES 6

½ pound pitted Medjool dates
4 ounces soft goat cheese, room
   temperature

2 tablespoons lemon zest
¼ teaspoon salt
¼ teaspoon ground culinary lavender

1. Slice each date lengthwise to make an opening without cutting all the way through. Set aside.
2. In a small bowl, stir together cheese, zest, salt, and lavender. Spoon an equal amount of the mixture into each date. Serve immediately or refrigerate.

POTATOES AU GRATIN CASSEROLE

*Everyone loves cheesy potatoes, but especially sensual Taureans. Cosmic
bulls understand that cheesy potatoes are the perfect companion to any
buffet table, for any occasion, and at any time of the day. This recipe
is vegan, which can appease all partygoers; however, if you know your
audience and you'd like to incorporate cheese, have at it! Either way, this
potato casserole is full of flavor and visually enticing. Gooey on the inside
with a crispy layer of bread crumbs on top, this one's likely to
disappear fast. So be sure you save yourself a spoonful,
luxurious Taurus, before it's too late!*

SERVES 4

4 medium potatoes
1 medium onion, peeled and chopped
1 tablespoon vegan margarine
2 tablespoons all-purpose flour
1½ cups unsweetened soy milk
2 teaspoons onion powder
1 teaspoon garlic powder

2 tablespoons nutritional yeast
1 teaspoon lemon juice
½ teaspoon salt
½ teaspoon paprika
⅛ teaspoon ground black pepper
¾ cup vegan bread crumbs

1. Preheat oven to 375°F.
2. Slice potatoes into thin coins and arrange half of the slices in a casserole or
   baking dish. Layer half of the onion on top of the potatoes.
3. In a small saucepan over low heat, melt margarine and then add flour, stirring
   to make a paste. Add soy milk, onion powder, garlic powder, nutritional yeast,
   lemon juice, and salt, stirring to combine. Stir until the sauce has thickened.
4. Pour half of the sauce over potatoes and onion, then layer remaining potatoes
   and onion on top of the sauce. Pour the remaining sauce on top.
5. Sprinkle with paprika and pepper and top with bread crumbs.
6. Cover and bake 45 minutes; then bake uncovered an additional 10 minutes.
   Allow to cool at least 10 minutes before serving; sauce will thicken as it cools.

TIRAMISU

Indulgent Tauruses adore the decadence of Tiramisu. There's something deliciously sinful about a dessert that includes ladyfinger cookies dipped in coffee, sugar, and liqueur—and then layered with velvety cream. For sensual Tauruses, dessert rivals sex as their favorite activity. All factors considered, this Tiramisu just might take the cake. After a big meal, comfortable Taurus needs a seriously convincing excuse to get moving again. A coffee-infused dessert will always do the trick for these celestial foodies. In fact, "Tiramisu" translates to "pick me up" in Italian!

SERVES 10

3 large eggs, separated
⅛ teaspoon ground nutmeg
¼ cup granulated sugar, divided
1 cup mascarpone cheese
½ cup strong black coffee, freshly made

6 tablespoons marsala or coffee liqueur
16 ladyfinger cookies, divided
2 tablespoons cocoa powder

1. In a medium bowl, whisk egg yolks, nutmeg, and 2 tablespoons sugar until the mixture thickens. Stir in mascarpone.
2. In a separate medium bowl, beat egg whites until stiff peaks form. Gently fold the mascarpone mixture into egg whites. Set aside.
3. In another medium bowl, add remaining sugar, coffee, and marsala. Stir the mixture until sugar is dissolved.
4. Dip eight ladyfingers, one at a time, into the coffee mixture for 1 second, then place them in a 6" × 10" × 4" baking dish. Don't leave ladyfingers in the coffee mixture for more than a second or they will become mushy.
5. Spread half of the mascarpone filling over ladyfingers. Dip remaining ladyfingers one at a time in the coffee mixture for 1 second, then place them in the dish over filling. Spread remaining mascarpone filling over ladyfingers. Cover and refrigerate 8 hours or overnight.
6. Sprinkle with cocoa powder before serving. Serve cold or at room temperature.

CAKE DOUGHNUTS

Tauruses love doughnuts and they love cake, but what about homemade Cake Doughnuts? The answer is a resounding "yes, please." These pan-fried doughnuts are supereasy to make, which is deliciously convenient for leisurely Taurus. Soft in the middle and crispy on the outside, these doughnuts are ideal for simple-pleasure-seeking foodies. When the doughnuts are fresh out of the frying pan, roll them in cinnamon sugar or dip in confectioners' sugar. Or, take it to next-level luxurious by glazing them with a chocolate ganache. The stars predict that your stomach will never steer you wrong, dear Taurus.

YIELDS 18 DOUGHNUTS

3 large eggs
¾ cup granulated sugar
¼ cup brown sugar
1 cup buttermilk
1 teaspoon vanilla extract
¼ cup butter, melted

3 cups all-purpose flour
¼ teaspoon salt
1 teaspoon baking powder
1 teaspoon baking soda
½ teaspoon ground nutmeg
3 cups corn oil

1. In a medium bowl, beat eggs until light. Gradually add sugars, beating until light and fluffy. Add buttermilk, vanilla, and butter and mix well.
2. In a sifter, combine flour, salt, baking powder, baking soda, and nutmeg, and sift over the batter; stir in. You may need to add more flour to make a soft dough.
3. On a floured surface, roll out dough to 1/3" thickness. Cut with doughnut cutter.
4. In a large skillet, heat oil to 375°F (use a cooking thermometer for best results). Carefully add four doughnuts; fry on both sides, turning once, until golden brown, about 3–4 minutes for each side. Repeat with remaining dough. Fry doughnut holes 1–2 minutes on each side. Serve.

MUDSLIDE

Gourmet Taureans love dessert, especially when dessert involves chocolate—and vodka. The Mudslide is the perfect cocktail for posh celestial bulls—expertly combining coffee and Irish liqueurs into one dreamy infusion that these bulls can't refuse. This boozy milkshake is here to help you take brunch to the next level, Taurus, so go ahead and pair this Mudslide with the Raspberry Waffles (see recipe in this chapter) for a seriously sensual experience. The Mudslide is here to help hedonistic Taureans sweeten up any day, so break out the whipped cream and prepare to be enamored!

SERVES 1

1 ounce vodka
½ ounce coffee liqueur
½ ounce Irish cream

Half-and-half to fill
Chocolate syrup and whipped cream (if frozen), for garnish

1. This drink can be made on the rocks or frozen. If making on the rocks, pour vodka, coffee liqueur, Irish cream, and half-and-half into a short glass of ice. Pour into a shaker. Shake and pour back into the glass. Serve.
2. If making frozen, pour the same ingredients into a blender with a cup of ice. Blend, then pour into a tall chocolate-swirled glass and top off with whipped cream. Serve.

Gemini:
The Adventurous Chef

Gemini, you're the wordsmith of the zodiac. Quick on your toes and even faster to retort, you're the brain everyone wants on their trivia team. As the first of the air signs, you thrive in the mental realm, and doubly so with fast-moving Mercury (planet of communication and thought) as your ruler. Speaking of double, you're symbolized by the twins, alluding to the two hemispheres of your brain and your ability to entertain multiple points of view at once. Are you being serious? Usually, no, but sometimes it's hard to tell! As the mutable air sign, you're a brilliant weaver of words. You keep it light and you make everyone laugh, which is why you are so adored!

Gemini, you possess a youthful sparkle and an unending curiosity, which leads you to invent new pathways in life, and also in the kitchen! You're capable of creating marvelous concoctions that keep us guessing, though you also love a dish with a story behind it. Adventurous and witty, you will take on any dish that amuses you. Habitually gabbing while you nosh, it's no wonder you never clear your plate. Your ideal dish is vibrant, thought-provoking, and nutrient-dense so that you can fill up in a few bites and meander elsewhere.

BANANA NUT-STUFFED FRENCH TOAST

Gemini, it's hard for you to sit still (especially once you've had your morning coffee), but if there's one dish that will convince you to stick around for breakfast, it's French toast! Witty Geminis will adore this delicious banana nut version—served with fresh raspberries and bursting with vitamins and minerals, what's not to love?! Start your day with these tasty breakfast triangles, and you'll have all the brainpower you crave to charge through your morning. And lucky for you, antsy Gemini, this recipe takes no time to whip up.

SERVES 4

6 large eggs
1½ cups milk
1 teaspoon vanilla extract
1 tablespoon brown sugar
½ teaspoon ground cinnamon
2 teaspoons canola oil, divided

8 slices day-old whole-wheat bread
2 medium bananas, peeled and sliced
1 cup chopped walnuts
Handful fresh raspberries, for garnish
Confectioners' sugar, for garnish

1. In a medium bowl, whisk together eggs, milk, vanilla, brown sugar, and cinnamon.
2. Heat 1 teaspoon canola oil in a large skillet over medium heat. Dip four slices of bread in the egg mixture and immediately add to the skillet and fry in canola oil until golden, about 3–4 minutes per side. Set aside.
3. Add remaining canola oil to skillet, dip remaining four slices of bread into the egg mixture and add to the skillet and fry until golden. Divide banana slices and walnuts evenly among the four slices of cooked bread in the skillet. Place reserved slices on top of the bananas to create four sandwiches.
4. Flip the sandwiches over and fry until heated through, about 3 minutes.
5. Halve the French toast diagonally and arrange slices on a platter. Scatter raspberries over the French toast triangles and sprinkle with confectioners' sugar.

LEMON POPPY SEED SMOOTHIE

You love a lemon poppy seed muffin, Gemini, but what about a smoothie? At the very least, your curiosity is piqued by this lemony creation—which is good, because the more interesting the smoothie, the more appealing it is to you. Vanilla yogurt lends this slightly unexpected concoction a dreamy creaminess and boosts the bright notes of the lemon. Eating these powerful omega-rich poppy seeds is likely to produce major taste bud euphoria. Enjoy this chilled treat after a long bike ride or while you recover from a lengthy cram session.

YIELDS 1½ CUPS

2 teaspoons poppy seeds
Juice and zest of 1 large lemon
1 cup low-fat vanilla yogurt

2 tablespoons raw honey
½ cup low-fat milk
½ cup ice

---

1. Combine all the ingredients in a blender and purée until smooth.
2. Serve immediately.

○ ○ ○ ○ NUTS AND SEEDS ○ ○ ○ ○

Gemini's active mind is constantly reading, listening to podcasts, and scrolling through social media for fun factoids and gossip. Nuts and seeds are packed with healthy fats and minerals that power your brain and nourish your nervous system. All the reason you need to eat more of them, intelligent Gemini!

EGGS FLORENTINE

Need a reason to stick around for breakfast? Of course you do, restless Gemini! This time go with a high-protein savory dish served hot from your oven. And since you love fun facts, brainy Gemini: "Florentine" refers to "spinach." Why? Queen of France, Catherine de' Medici, brought spinach from Florence to France. If you have more time to spare, crafty Gemini, you can skip the microwave and make your Florentine mixture in a saucepan instead.

SERVES 2

1 English muffin
2 large eggs
5 ounces chopped frozen spinach
1 tablespoon low-fat mayonnaise

1 teaspoon salt
1 teaspoon ground black pepper
2 teaspoons shredded cheese of your choice

1. Preheat oven to 350°F. Split muffin open and place on a baking sheet.
2. Crack an egg onto each muffin half. Bake 10 minutes.
3. Meanwhile, place spinach in a medium microwave-safe bowl and heat in the microwave until soft and warm, about 2 minutes.
4. Add mayonnaise, salt, and pepper to spinach. Stir together.
5. Remove muffins and top with the spinach mixture. Add 1 teaspoon shredded cheese to each half and serve.

○ ○ ○ ○ DON'T FORGET TO FUEL YOURSELF ○ ○ ○ ○

As a Gemini, you may feel that your brain needs more feeding than your stomach; in fact, it's easy for you to forget to eat (something your neighbors, Taurus and Cancer, could never understand). You'll often know you're hungry because you're tired. Prevent that feeling of "running on empty" by prioritizing high-powered foods and healthy fats in your diet.

FALAFEL PITAS

As an air sign, you tend to gravitate toward light, airy, crispy, and crunchy foods. You've replaced a meal with chips far more often than you'd like to admit. But the reality is that breezy Gemini needs foods that are nutritiously substantial. So here's your fast-food alternative: falafel. Never heard of it? You're missing out. Falafel is a Middle Eastern mini fritter, fried up with mashed chickpeas, parsley, and spices. This sandwich offers you high-protein chickpeas in two ways (falafel and hummus)—something your dual nature is sure to appreciate. So why not bring this anytime meal to a lunch box near you?

SERVES 6

2 cups cooked chickpeas
1 tablespoon baking powder
1 medium onion, peeled and sliced
4 cloves garlic
¼ cup chopped fresh Italian parsley
1 teaspoon ground cumin
1 teaspoon ground coriander
½ teaspoon salt

½ teaspoon ground black pepper
¼ cup all-purpose flour
Canola oil, for frying
1 cup classic hummus
6 whole-wheat or regular pita pockets
1 medium cucumber, sliced
1 large tomato, cored and sliced

1. Place chickpeas, baking powder, onion, garlic, parsley, cumin, coriander, salt, and pepper in a food processor. Pulse on high until a paste forms.
2. Scrape the paste into a large bowl. Stir in flour. Cover and refrigerate 1 hour.
3. Heat 1" canola oil in a large skillet over medium-high heat. Roll the chickpea mixture into 1"–2" balls and fry until golden on all sides, about 5 minutes. Drain on paper towel–lined plates.
4. Spread some hummus into each pita pocket. Add cucumber and tomato. Stuff with falafel and serve.

CHICKEN CHERRY SALAD SANDWICHES

You're unafraid to go bold when you mix and match, playful Gemini. In this recipe, the chicken salad you know and love takes an eccentric and slightly sweet swivel with the addition of red cherries. For those times when you're tempted to just eat a juicy piece of fruit, but you really need a sandwich, here's a lunchtime nosh that expertly combines forces and satisfies each of your dueling twins' tastes. With fresh onion and lettuce, this sandwich offers you the crunch that air signs crave. Cherries and chicken are a combo most people are missing out on, but not you, inventive Gemini!

SERVES 4

- 1½ pounds poached chicken breast, cubed
- ½ medium Vidalia onion, peeled and diced
- ⅔ cup halved fresh sweet cherries
- ¼ cup mayonnaise
- 2 tablespoons tarragon vinegar
- ¼ teaspoon celery seed
- ¼ teaspoon sea salt
- ¼ teaspoon ground white pepper
- ¼ teaspoon dried summer savory
- 4 Boston lettuce leaves
- 4 whole-wheat or white kaiser rolls
- 1 medium avocado, peeled, pitted, and sliced

1. In a medium bowl, combine chicken, onion, cherries, mayonnaise, vinegar, celery seed, salt, pepper, and summer savory until all the ingredients are evenly distributed.
2. Place a lettuce leaf on the bottom half of each roll. Evenly distribute the chicken salad among the rolls. Top each with avocado slices. Close the sandwiches and serve.

MILK AND OAT BARS

Energy bars are a major staple in every air sign's diet, but especially yours, free-styling Gemini. So, here's a fantastic DIY energy bar recipe with big flavor and minus all the wrappers (which as you know are terrible for the environment). This recipe is packed with superfoods to sustain knowledgeable Gemini's high brain bandwidth between meals—or even substitute for breakfast in a pinch. Coconut digests slowly, for sustainable energy, while ginger warms and energizes. Be sure to keep one of these in your bag for when you need a little extra brain power.

--- **YIELDS 12 BARS** ---

14 ounces sweetened condensed milk

2⅓ cups old-fashioned rolled oats

1 cup raw almonds

¾ cup unsweetened dried cherries, cranberries, or blueberries

¾ cup shredded unsweetened coconut

¼ teaspoon sea salt

¼ teaspoon ground ginger

1 teaspoon vanilla extract

1. Preheat oven to 250°F. Oil an 11" × 7" baking pan.
2. In a medium saucepan, heat condensed milk over medium-low heat. Do not boil. Stir in the remaining ingredients.
3. Pour the mixture into prepared pan. Flatten with the back of a spoon or spatula, taking care the mixture reaches all four corners of the pan.
4. Bake 60–70 minutes or until the mixture looks dry but is not browned. The mixture should be only slightly sticky at this point. Remove pan from oven and place on a wire rack. Allow the mixture to cool completely in the pan.
5. Use a large, flat spatula to invert the contents of the pan onto a cutting board. Slice into twelve equal-sized bars. Store in an airtight container.

∘ ∘ ∘ ∘ **THE METHOD TO YOUR MADNESS** ∘ ∘ ∘ ∘

Curious Gemini, you might be wondering if the long bake time on these bars is a typo. We assure you, it is not. Energy bars are baked low and slow to preserve the nutrients in the dish and prevent drying out. Think ahead and bake these before hunger strikes.

MARINATED BEEF SKEWERS

Crafty Geminis are adept with their hands, so they'll have as much fun assembling these beef skewers as they will eating them! High in protein and even bigger in flavor, these crunchy, garlicky handhelds are the perfect appetizer for brainy Gemini. Walnuts supply vital nutrients to the brain, while also delivering a perfect amount of texture to these kebabs. If you are using wooden skewers here, be sure to soak them for no less than 1 hour before baking. Creative Geminis might also like to add peppers and onions (or whatever!) to their skewers, but we'll leave that up to you!

SERVES 10

2½ pounds sirloin beef, cut into 1"–1½" cubes
½ cup walnuts
½ bulb roasted peeled garlic

¼ cup olive oil
½ cup dry red wine
1 teaspoon ground black pepper

1. Skewer beef cubes. Place the skewers in a single layer in a baking dish large enough for the skewers to lie flat.
2. In a blender, finely grind walnuts, then add garlic cloves, oil, wine, and pepper. Blend completely.
3. Pour the sauce over the beef skewers in the dish, making sure to coat beef completely. Marinate beef in the refrigerator no longer than 2 hours (the acid in the wine will "cook" the meat if left in too long).
4. Preheat oven to 400°F. Roast the skewers 10–15 minutes. Serve hot.

SWEET POTATO FRITTERS

Versatile Gemini needs freedom for spontaneity, so when it comes to kitchen concoctions, sweet potatoes are your kind of root vegetable. Infinitely inventive and curious, your craftiness pulls through for you again, Gemini, when you repurpose last night's mashed sweet potatoes into fritters. Slightly browned and crispy on the outside, and gooey on the inside, this is one dish you'll love to bite into at any time of the day. While there are about a million ways to enjoy a sweet potato, theses ones have a spicy kick!
Top with a spoonful of sour cream and enjoy!

SERVES 4

2½ cups mashed sweet potatoes
1 large egg, beaten
1 medium onion, peeled and diced
1 medium jalapeño, seeded and diced

1 teaspoon Cajun seasoning
1 teaspoon fresh thyme leaves
½ cup fresh bread crumbs
Oil, for frying

1. In a large bowl, mix together all the ingredients, except the oil, until thoroughly combined. Form into 2"–2½" balls.
2. Heat ¼" oil in a large skillet over medium heat. Add the fritters to oil and cook each fritter until browned on both sides, about 8 minutes. Drain on paper towel–lined plates. Serve.

GOLDEN WEST CHILI

"Hominy." It's not just a word that might come in handy while playing Words with Friends, intellectual Gemini; it's also a delicious corn kernel you want in your chili. Hominy boasts large, soft kernels, and it's not sweet like typical yellow corn. Instead, its mild flavor compares to white rice. Gemini, you might be a star student, but you're also the life of the party. This dish calls for an entire can of beer, so you can feel both sophisticated and mischievous as you pour. Use soy crumbles as directed or, if you're feeling adventurous, substitute them with carne molida.

SERVES 6

3 tablespoons vegetable oil
1 large onion, peeled and diced
12 ounces ground soy "meat" crumbles
1 tablespoon chili powder
1 (15-ounce) can golden hominy
1 (15.5-ounce) can canary beans, drained and rinsed
1 (15.5-ounce) can pigeon peas, drained and rinsed
1 cup green salsa
1 cup Mexican beer, or more as needed
⅛ teaspoon salt

⅛ teaspoon ground black pepper
3 medium tomatillos, chopped, for garnish
½ cup grated Cheddar cheese, for garnish
½ cup chopped fresh cilantro, for garnish
½ cup diced, peeled, pitted avocados, for garnish
¼ cup toasted pumpkin seeds, for garnish

1. In a large saucepan over medium heat, heat oil and sauté onion until partially golden, about 5 minutes.
2. Add soy "meat" crumbles and continue cooking 3–4 minutes. Stir in chili powder. Add hominy, beans, pigeon peas, salsa, and beer and stir well.
3. Reduce heat to medium-low and continue cooking and stirring, about 8 minutes. Season with salt and pepper.
4. Serve in individual bowls, garnishing with tomatillos, cheese, cilantro, avocado, and pumpkin seeds.

BIBIMBAP
(Korean Mixed Rice with Meat and Vegetables)

Lighthearted and playful Gemini will love everything about this colorful Korean rice bowl. Distinguished by gochugaru (chili powder) and runny eggs, bibimbap is as enjoyable for celestial wordsmiths to eat as it is to say! You'll love the versatility here, Gemini, as any vegetables are welcome. Your agile mind is beyond capable of multitasking the moving parts in this recipe (you love a good puzzle), but overall, bibimbap is a very easy dish to make. And once you get a bite, witty Gemini, the stars predict that this Bibimbap will be a permanent addition to your own vernacular as well!

SERVES 4

4 ounces lean ground beef
1 tablespoon soy sauce
2 cloves garlic, minced
1 teaspoon brown sugar
1 teaspoon sesame oil
2 tablespoons vegetable oil, divided
1 medium carrot, peeled and julienned
¾ teaspoon salt, divided

½ pint shiitake mushrooms, sliced
½ medium zucchini, thinly sliced
4 large eggs
4 cups cooked medium-grain rice
½ cup Sigeumchi Namul (see sidebar)
½ cup blanched mung bean sprouts
1 tablespoon gochugaru or red pepper flakes

1. In a medium bowl, add ground beef, soy sauce, garlic, brown sugar, and sesame oil. Mix well to combine.
2. In a large skillet over medium heat, add the beef mixture and cook until thoroughly browned, about 10 minutes. Transfer beef to a bowl and set aside.
3. Return skillet to the heat and add 1 teaspoon vegetable oil. Once oil shimmers add carrot and cook, stirring constantly until tender, about 3 minutes. Season with ¼ teaspoon salt. Remove from pan and set aside.

4. Return skillet to the heat and add 1 teaspoon vegetable oil. Once oil shimmers, add mushrooms and cook, stirring constantly until tender, about 3 minutes. Season with ¼ teaspoon salt. Remove from pan and set aside.

5. Return skillet to the heat and add 1 teaspoon vegetable oil. Once oil shimmers, add zucchini and cook, stirring constantly until tender, about 3 minutes. Season with ¼ teaspoon salt. Remove from pan and set aside.

6. Return skillet to the heat and add 1 teaspoon vegetable oil. Once oil shimmers, add eggs. Cook until the edges of the whites are set, then cover the pan with a lid and cook 1 minute or until the whites are set but the yolks are still soft. Remove from pan and set aside.

7. Return skillet to the heat and increase heat to high. Add remaining vegetable oil and once it shimmers add rice. Press rice down so it forms a flat disk. Cook until rice is golden brown on the bottom, about 5 minutes. Divide rice among four serving bowls.

8. Add vegetables, beef, Sigeumchi Namul, and mung bean sprouts around the edges of the bowls. Place a fried egg in the center of each portion and garnish with gochugaru or red pepper flakes. Serve immediately.

∘ ∘ ∘ ∘ SIGEUMCHI NAMUL ∘ ∘ ∘ ∘
(Korean Seasoned Spinach)

To make Korean Seasoned Spinach you'll need 1 teaspoon salt, ½ pound fresh spinach, 2 teaspoons toasted sesame oil, 1 minced clove garlic, 1 thinly sliced green onion, and ½ teaspoon toasted sesame seeds. Bring 2 quarts water and salt to a boil over high heat and add spinach. Cook 30 seconds. Remove spinach from water and rinse under cool water to stop the cooking. Drain spinach well. Pat dry with paper towels. Cut the spinach into 1" pieces with a knife and add to a large bowl along with the remaining ingredients. Toss to coat and serve. Serves 4.

TABBOULEH

Did you know that parsley is a natural breath freshener? Lucky for you, fast-talking Gemini, parsley builds the base of this Middle Eastern salad, along with bulgur wheat, which makes this salad both filling and satisfying to eat on its own. That said, brainy Gemini, you'd be smart to pair this with your falafel and hummus recipes to take your meals to the next level. Parsley also aids with digestion, which is perfect for those times when you accidentally skip lunch and your stomach is sassing you.

SERVES 6

1 cup cracked (bulgur) wheat
1 small cucumber, peeled and chopped
3 medium scallions, finely chopped (ends trimmed)
2 medium tomatoes, cored, seeded, and chopped
2 tablespoons chopped fresh chives

1 cup chopped fresh Italian parsley
½ cup extra-virgin olive oil
Juice of 2 medium lemons (about ½ cup)
⅛ teaspoon salt
⅛ teaspoon ground black pepper

1. Soak wheat in 1 quart water for 15 minutes (or overnight). Drain and squeeze out excess moisture by tying up in a cheesecloth or clean kitchen towel.
2. In a large bowl, combine wheat with cucumber, scallions, tomatoes, chives, and parsley. Dress with olive oil, lemon juice, salt, and pepper.
3. Set aside to marinate 2–3 hours before serving.

CASHEW CHICKEN

Gemini craves a dinner as adventurous as they are. That's why you need to try Cashew Chicken—a spicy stir-fry served over a bed of jasmine rice. This dish carries all the signature Thai flavors you love. Yes, it's a known fact that restless Geminis adore sampling cuisines from all over the world and will try anything (and we mean anything) once. However, this spicy Cashew Chicken is sure to be a regular in your house, fun-loving Gemini!

SERVES 4

2 tablespoons vegetable oil
¼ cup Thai dried chilies, chopped into ½"-long pieces
½ tablespoon minced garlic
½ pound boneless, skinless chicken breasts, sliced into strips
1 small onion, peeled and sliced into 1" pieces
½ cup fried or roasted cashews

1 cup chopped red bell pepper
1½ tablespoons fish sauce
1 tablespoon dark soy sauce
1 tablespoon granulated sugar
½ teaspoon salt
⅓ cup chopped green onion
Cilantro, for garnish
2 cups cooked jasmine rice

1. Heat a deep sauté pan or a wok until hot. Add vegetable oil and fry chilies until they just change color, about 1 minute. Keep moving chilies around or they will burn. Remove chilies from oil and set aside.
2. Add minced garlic and fry over medium heat until golden, about 10 seconds. Add chicken and sauté until almost cooked, about 1–2 minutes. Add onion, cashews, fried chilies, and bell pepper and stir-fry about 1–2 minutes.
3. Season with fish sauce, soy sauce, sugar, and salt. Add green onion and fold until onions are wilted, about 30 seconds–1 minute. Turn off the heat. Garnish with cilantro and serve over rice.

∘ ∘ ∘ ∘ **CULINARY TRIVIA** ∘ ∘ ∘ ∘

Geminis love to try exotic dishes, so why not hold an international dinner party for your family and friends and have everyone bring a dish from another culture? Such an exciting dining adventure would be right up your alley, bold Gemini, and it might help bring some of your more timid friends out of their shells too!

SHRIMP SHIITAKE POT STICKERS

Dexterous Geminis will love folding up these pan-fried dumplings as much as they will love eating them! This recipe makes more dumplings than you could possibly eat in one sitting, so plan on freezing leftovers or wow your friends by serving them up at your next party. Shrimp is the featured protein here, but adventurous Geminis will surely delight in experimenting with others.

SERVES 25

1 large egg
1 bunch scallions, minced and ends trimmed, plus some sliced scallions for garnish
4 fresh shiitake mushrooms, minced
2 medium heads baby bok choy, finely chopped
1 pound raw shrimp, peeled, deveined, and minced

2 tablespoons sesame oil
2 tablespoons soy sauce
2 tablespoons grated ginger
1½ tablespoons grated garlic
1½ tablespoons cornstarch
1 teaspoon ground black pepper
50 round dumpling wrappers
Canola oil, for frying
5 cups water

1. In a large bowl, combine egg, scallions, mushrooms, bok choy, shrimp, sesame oil, soy sauce, ginger, garlic, cornstarch, and pepper to form a uniform mixture.
2. Place a dumpling wrapper on a plate or clean, dry surface. Place 1 teaspoon filling in the center of wrapper. Fold wrapper in half to form a half-moon shape, pinching the wrapper tightly together.
3. Press the "fold" side gently down on the plate so it can stand alone, seam-side up. Repeat until all filling and wrappers are gone.
4. Heat a small amount of canola oil in a large saucepan over medium heat. Place about ten pot stickers flat-side down and fry until the bottom is browned. Add 1 cup water, cover immediately. Allow dumplings to steam about 5–10 minutes.
5. Once dumplings are fully cooked the water will have fully evaporated and the bottoms will be crisp. Repeat for remaining dumplings. Garnish with a sprinkle of scallion slices. Serve with sauce of your choice.

CHEDDAR CHEESE FONDUE

Geminis love fondue—both chocolate and cheesy. This time, though, we're going savory with Cheddar cheese dip. Geminis get bored just standing around at parties, so this is the perfect fun and interactive dip to bring both entertainment and deliciousness to Gemini's social sphere. If you have a fondue set, wonderful. If not, improvisational Gemini can utilize a slow cooker. Or go ahead and use a saucepan if you get desperate. Geminis will adore dipping bread, soft pretzel pieces, or fruits and vegetables in their cheesy fondue. Get creative and have fun with this one, witty Gemini!

SERVES 6

2 tablespoons butter
1 medium onion, peeled and chopped
3 cloves garlic, minced
2 tablespoons all-purpose flour
¼ teaspoon salt
⅛ teaspoon ground white pepper
2 cups chicken stock
1 cup 1% milk
1 (8-ounce) package low-fat cream
   cheese, cubed

1½ cups shredded Cheddar cheese
2 cups baby carrots, for dipping
3 medium apples, peeled, cored, and
   sliced, for dipping
2 medium green bell peppers, seeded
   and sliced, for dipping
3 cups cubed French bread, for dipping

1. In a large saucepan over medium heat, melt butter. Add onion and garlic; cook and stir 5 minutes. Sprinkle with flour, salt, and pepper and cook until bubbly, about 3–4 minutes.
2. Add stock and milk; cook and stir until the mixture starts to thicken. Add cream cheese; cook and stir until melted and blended. Add Cheddar cheese; cook and stir until blended.
3. Pour the mixture into a fondue pot and light the base. Serve immediately with the remaining ingredients.

NECTARINE UPSIDE-DOWN CAKE

Gemini, your versatile mind darts in all directions, but for dessert, you're going deliciously upside down! Upside-down cakes are characterized by their delectable caramelized glaze enveloping their moist interior. In upside-down cakes, the fruit pieces are usually laid in the pan first so that they turn out on top when served. Geminis adore the tart, juicy nectarines featured in this tasty cake. Don't be shy when greasing the pan, agile Gemini; you want that cake flip to be as elegant as you.

SERVES 10

½ cup unsalted butter, at room temperature, divided
½ cup light brown sugar
1 large egg, at room temperature
1 teaspoon vanilla extract
1 cup all-purpose flour

1 teaspoon baking powder
¼ teaspoon salt
⅓ cup buttermilk
¼ cup demerara sugar
2 cups sliced nectarines

1. Preheat oven to 350°F.
2. In a large bowl, cream together 7 tablespoons butter and brown sugar. Once combined, add egg and vanilla; beat thoroughly.
3. In a medium bowl, whisk together flour, baking powder, and salt.
4. Add buttermilk and the flour mixture to the butter mixture alternately, beginning and ending with the flour mixture. The batter should be very fluffy.
5. Use remaining tablespoon butter to coat the bottom and sides of an 8" × 8" baking pan. Sprinkle sugar over butter, and then top with nectarine slices. Pour the batter over the nectarines.
6. Bake 40 minutes or until a toothpick inserted in the middle comes out with a few moist but not wet crumbs.
7. Cool completely on a wire rack. Invert onto a platter to serve upside down.

CHOCOLATE CHIP BANANA CAKE

Versatile Geminis will go bananas for this Chocolate Chip Banana Cake. What to do with those seemingly inedible mushy bananas? Inventive Gemini uses their kitchen magician skills to transform them into a dessert most appealing. In fact, the mushier the bananas, the tastier your cake will be, improvisational Gemini. You love dessert, Gemini, so why settle for banana bread when you can have banana cake? Chocolate chips are one of the key pieces that elevate this tasty treat to cake pedestal status. Fact: Chocolate Chip Banana Cake is a perfect dessert, but you'll convince yourself that it's also a fabulous breakfast, smooth-talking Gemini!

SERVES 9

¾ cup whole-wheat flour
¾ cup all-purpose flour
1 teaspoon baking powder
¼ teaspoon baking soda
¾ cup granulated sugar
⅛ teaspoon salt

⅔ cup dark chocolate chips
⅔ cup mashed ripe bananas
⅓ cup unsweetened applesauce
⅓ cup fat-free plain yogurt
2 large eggs
1 teaspoon banana extract

1. Preheat oven to 350°F.
2. In a large bowl, combine flours, baking powder, baking soda, sugar, salt, and chocolate chips and stir well.
3. Add the remaining ingredients; stir until smooth.
4. Pour the batter into an 8" square pan. Bake 30 minutes. Cool and cut into nine squares.

SIDECAR

You may be playful, but you're serious about your mixed drinks. This classic Prohibition-era cocktail is exactly what Gemini craves when it's time to get your drink on. Orangey Cointreau combines with lemon juice for a brandy martini that's refreshingly tart, yet sweet enough to satisfy dueling sides of your palate, twinning Gemini. You want a cocktail that's popular enough to be good, but fringy enough to be savvy. So go with the Sidecar—a drink that will never steer you wrong!

SERVES 1

2 ounces brandy
½ ounce Cointreau

1 ounce fresh lemon juice

Combine the ingredients in a shaker nearly filled with ice. Shake and strain into a cocktail glass.

Cancer:
The Mood Chef

That tough outer shell of yours will fool some, but not all, dear Cancer crab. Once you feel comfortable enough to emerge from your shell, you reveal a sensitive and compassionate soul. As a water sign, you interpret the world according to your feelings. Cancers are psychic sponges, soaking up impressions of their environment. At any point Cancer feels uncomfortable, they simply retreat into their shell, which is more than a protective mechanism; it's this cosmic crustacean's home! Cancers tend to be homebodies. So if a Cancer invites you over, lucky you! The home is where Cancers get to showcase their natural caretaking instincts.

Ruled by the Moon, Cancers have some of the best memories of the zodiac, and they love a warm, fuzzy trip down memory lane. In the kitchen, Cancers are always intuitively guided by how they feel. They love re-creating nostalgic recipes shared with loved ones, like the Chicken Potpie recipe in this chapter. So without further ado, here's a feel-good menu designed to nourish you, Cancer—complete with nostalgic recipes that are sure to give you those comfy-home vibes even when you're on the go!

EASY
SWEET CREPES

Nothing says "snuggly Sunday morning" like a fresh batch of crepes, so here's the perfect excuse to sleep in and stay in your pajamas all morning, cozy Cancer. These fluffy crepes are sure to satisfy whimsical Cancer, as the possibilities for crepe fillings are truly endless! Strawberries and chocolate are a perfect sweet tooth satisfier, or go with bananas, cinnamon, and high-protein almond butter following your yoga class. You always go with what you feel, sensitive Cancer, so let the mood of the morning guide you.

--- **YIELDS 10 CREPES** ---

1 large egg
¼ cup liquid egg substitute
4 large egg whites
½ cup orange juice
¾ cup skim milk
3 tablespoons butter, melted

½ cup all-purpose flour
½ cup whole-wheat flour
2 tablespoons granulated sugar
¼ teaspoon salt
2 teaspoons vanilla extract

1. In a large bowl, combine egg, egg substitute, and egg whites; beat until frothy. Add orange juice, milk, and butter and beat well.
2. Add flours, sugar, salt, and vanilla and beat until smooth. Let the batter stand for 30 minutes.
3. Spray a 7" crepe pan with nonstick cooking spray. Place over medium heat. Pour 3 tablespoons batter onto the hot pan. Immediately lift the pan and swirl so the batter evenly coats the bottom.
4. Cook 60–70 seconds or until you can pick up the crepe. Carefully flip the crepe and cook on the second side 45 seconds. Invert onto a clean kitchen towel. Repeat with the remaining batter. Do not stack crepes when cool; separate each with some waxed paper. Fill with desired toppings. Serve.

SAUSAGE AND MUSHROOM OMELET

How you start your morning sets the tone for the whole day, moody crustacean, so it's super important that you get a stellar breakfast! Cancers can never go wrong with a savory Sausage and Mushroom Omelet—the half-moon-shaped special that can be enjoyed anytime, and no matter the phase of the Moon! This high-protein omelet features lean turkey sausage, mushrooms, and egg whites. Cancerians are more particular about their food rituals than any other sign, which is why cheese and hot sauce are always optional, dear Cancer.

SERVES 2

4 large egg whites
1 large whole egg
¼ teaspoon salt
1 tablespoon olive oil

½ cup chopped cooked turkey sausage
½ cup chopped mushrooms
½ cup diced green bell pepper
Parsley, for garnish

1. In a small bowl, beat egg whites and egg. Mix in salt.
2. In a small skillet over low heat, heat olive oil. Pour the egg mixture in to coat the surface. Cook until edges show firmness.
3. Add sausage, mushrooms, and peppers so that they cover the entire mixture evenly. Fold one side over the other to form a half-moon shape.
4. Flip the half-moon omelet so both sides are evenly cooked, about 1–2 minutes per side. Serve with a sprinkle of parsley.

PB&J SMOOTHIE

Fond memories of peanut butter and jelly sandwiches pleasantly smooshed in your school lunch box remind you of a time when life was simpler. Luckily, some things need not change. Well, not totally. Nostalgic Cancers can also enjoy this iconic flavor duo from a Mason jar. For those on-the-go days when you'd rather be at home, cozy Cancer, this is the perfect TLC smoothie to pack. Slightly tart and superjuicy, Concord grapes are some of the most flavorful grapes around. If you can't find seedless Concords, blend the grapes alone first and use a fine strainer to help you sort out the seed remnants.

YIELDS 1½ CUPS

2 cups Concord grapes
2 tablespoons smooth peanut butter

1½ cups almond milk
1 cup ice

1. Combine all the ingredients in a blender and purée until smooth.
2. Serve immediately.

○ ○ ○ ○ MEAL TIME = ZEN TIME ○ ○ ○ ○

Sweet Cancer, your mind-body connection is invaluable to you. Watery Cancers are cautioned against eating when they are upset, as it affects digestion. Make mealtime a pleasurable ritual. And whatever you do, do not multitask while you eat! Unlike their zodiac neighbors, Cancers are not big talkers while they munch, preferring to be present with every bite.

TOMATO AND PESTO GRILLED CHEESE PANINI

You're admittedly a creature of habit, nostalgic Cancer, so it's no wonder you frequently enjoy the same dishes you enjoyed as a child. That said, habitual Cancer, getting too comfortable in a routine isn't your style—which is why empathetic Cancers will love this flavorful twist on a favorite lunchtime nosh. Here, your iconic grilled cheese sandwich is elevated with a garlicky-basil pesto spread and a panini press. If you don't have a press, not to worry. Simply wrap foil underneath a full tea kettle and set it on top. Pesto is best enjoyed fresh but can always be prepared a day ahead.

SERVES 1

3 slices mozzarella cheese
2 slices Italian bread
2 slices tomato

1 tablespoon Traditional Pesto (see sidebar)

1. Preheat the panini press. Lay cheese on one bread slice. Add tomato and Traditional Pesto and cover with remaining bread slice.
2. Place the sandwich on the press, close the lid, and cook 3–5 minutes.
3. Remove from the press, cut in half, and serve warm.

∘ ∘ ∘ ∘ TRADITIONAL PESTO ∘ ∘ ∘ ∘

It's true you can buy jarred pesto at the store, but why not try making your own from scratch? This recipe will make 2 cups of pesto. Take 2 bunches fresh basil (chopped), 1/2 bulb garlic (chopped), 1/2 cup toasted pine nuts, and 1 cup extra-virgin olive oil. Then, in a food processor, pulse the basil, garlic, and pine nuts until well chopped and blended. Slowly pour in the oil and blend until relatively smooth. Use as desired.

CHICKEN POTPIE

What is your gut telling you, intuitive Cancer? It's lunchtime, so chances are it's telling you to eat Chicken Potpie—the quintessential dish made to nourish your soul on a rainy day. Sentimental Cancers will especially look forward to that first supersteamy, aromatic bite. Look for organic puff pastry for a fresher taste, though domestic Cancers might even prefer to make their own!

SERVES 6

1 tablespoon unsalted butter
1½ tablespoons olive oil
2 medium carrots, peeled and diced
2 medium parsnips, peeled and diced
1 medium turnip, diced
2 medium stalks celery, diced
1 medium onion, peeled and diced
1 medium shallot, peeled and minced
2 cloves garlic, minced
3 medium Yukon Gold potatoes, diced
½ cup all-purpose flour
2¾ cups chicken stock

1 bay leaf
1½ cups 2% milk
1 cup fresh or frozen peas
¾ cup fresh or frozen corn kernels
1 tablespoon minced sage
2 tablespoons minced fresh Italian parsley
1 teaspoon sea salt
1 teaspoon ground white pepper
1½ pounds cooked cubed chicken
1 sheet puff pastry
1 large egg, beaten

1. Preheat oven to 350°F.
2. Heat butter and oil in a large skillet over medium heat. Add carrots, parsnips, turnip, celery, onion, shallot, garlic, and potatoes and sauté until the vegetables are beginning to soften and onions and shallot are translucent, about 5–8 minutes. Sprinkle with flour and cook 2 minutes, stirring occasionally.
3. Add stock, bay leaf, and milk and simmer until the mixture reduces and thickens, about 15 minutes. Discard bay leaf.
4. Add peas, corn, sage, parsley, salt, pepper, and chicken. Continue to simmer 5 minutes.
5. Transfer mixture to an oven-safe 2-quart casserole dish. Top with puff pastry. Use a fork to pierce the pastry. Brush with beaten egg.
6. Bake 30 minutes or until the filling is piping hot and the pastry is golden brown. Serve immediately.

OATMEAL RAISIN SCONES

Emotive Cancers adore a plush pastry that's not too sweet but still hits the sweet spot midday. Made with rolled oats and butter for sustainable energy to get you through the afternoon, these Oatmeal Raisin Scones are the perfect treat for cozy Cancerians. Pair with afternoon tea or coffee, or even snag one as a light dessert after dinner. Bake time can be adjusted depending on how big you prefer your scones. Bake in rounds as instructed, or arrange in crescents for a slightly different scone experience—let your mood decide. Allow your culinary intuition to guide you, dreamy Moon child!

SERVES 6

1½ cups rolled oats, divided
½ cup all-purpose flour
2 tablespoons wheat germ
3 tablespoons granulated sugar
½ teaspoon salt
1⅛ teaspoons baking powder
6 tablespoons cold unsalted butter, cut in pieces

2 large eggs
⅔ cup buttermilk
½ teaspoon vanilla extract
1 cup raisins
1 large egg white
2 tablespoons raw sugar

1. Preheat oven to 400°F. Line a baking pan with parchment paper or spray lightly with oil. Grind half of the oats into flour in a food processor.
2. Combine remaining oats, oat flour, all-purpose flour, wheat germ, sugar, salt, baking powder, and butter in a food processor with a metal blade. Process until the mixture resembles cornmeal.
3. In a large bowl, whisk together eggs, buttermilk, and vanilla. Stir in raisins with a spatula or wooden spoon.
4. Add the dry ingredients and fold in with spatula. Drop scones in rounds onto prepared baking sheet.
5. Brush scones with egg white and sprinkle with raw sugar. Bake 15 minutes. Serve.

KALE WITH GARLIC AND THYME

Cosmic Cancer crabs will delight in this flavorful green dish. Kale is vastly abundant in vitamins and minerals, and since this side is so tasty, it will be hard to believe it's so healthy. Cooked vegetables are easiest on the digestion, so sensitive-stomached Cancers will appreciate that this recipe calls for boiling water. That said, if you'd like to preserve more of the kale's nutrients, steaming is another way to go. You'll notice your heap of greens cooks down to about an eighth of its size, allowing you to enjoy even more vegetables in every bite. Yum! Not a fan of kale yet? This dish will convert you, Cancer.

SERVES 4

2 pounds kale, stems and ribs removed
1 tablespoon olive oil
1 medium red onion, peeled and chopped
1 tablespoon chopped garlic
⅛ teaspoon crushed red pepper

2 teaspoons chopped fresh thyme leaves or ½ teaspoon dried
¼ cup dry sherry or white wine
⅛ teaspoon salt
⅛ teaspoon ground black pepper

1. Bring a large pot of well-salted water to a rolling boil. Add kale and cook 10 minutes until it has lost its waxy coating and the leaves are tender. Transfer to a colander to drain, reserving about ½ cup cooking liquid. Roughly chop kale.
2. Heat oil in a large skillet or Dutch oven. Add onion, garlic, red pepper, and thyme. Cook over medium heat until onions are soft and starting to brown around the edges, about 7–8 minutes.
3. Add sherry and cook 5 minutes until all alcohol has evaporated. Add kale and reserved liquid and cook 10 minutes more. Season with salt and pepper and serve.

FONDANT POTATOES AND PEARL ONIONS

Adorable Cancers can't resist the cute. Circles and spheres automatically signal "cute chubby baby" to the brain, and love is instant. Blame it on those nurturing instincts, Cancer. Doting crustaceans will surely fall in love with the teeny-tiny pearl onions (sooo cute!), but the melt-in-your-mouth creamy fondant potatoes are truly the stars of this stellar herbal dish. Expertly browned on the outside and pillow-soft on the inside, slow-roasted fondant potatoes are perhaps the most exquisite way to enjoy potatoes. Nurturing Cancers can pair this elegant appetizer with the Tarragon-Roasted Chicken (see recipe in this chapter) for a soul food dinner that's cosmically epic.

SERVES 6

2 pounds unpeeled baby potatoes
1 pound pearl onions, peeled
1 tablespoon unsalted butter
1 tablespoon olive oil

½ teaspoon sea salt
½ teaspoon ground black pepper
3 cups chicken stock
1 tablespoon herbes de Provence

1. Arrange potatoes and onions in the bottom of a large nonstick pan in a single layer. Add the remaining ingredients. Bring to a boil.
2. Reduce heat and partially cover with a lid. Continue to boil until much of the stock has evaporated, about 20 minutes. Potatoes should still be about half submerged in the stock at this point.
3. Use a wooden spoon to press down on each potato, cracking the skin. Continue to cook until all of the stock has completely evaporated and the bottoms of potatoes and onions are browned, about 10–25 minutes.
4. Flip potatoes and onions and cook the other side about 5 minutes. Use a large, flat spatula to remove potatoes and onions from the pan. Serve.

TOMATO SOUP WITH FRIED PASTA GARNISH

Most people have fond memories of eating this cherished soup, but especially you, nostalgic Cancer. This recipe features fragrant basil, garlic, and parsley—and it can be vegan if you omit the Parmesan cheese curls and pasta garnish. But if you're a cheese-loving celestial crab, just snag a vegetable peeler and a hard block of Parmesan cheese and curl away! The fried pasta delivers the perfect amount of crunch to this smooth, creamy dish. Your soup is the perfect companion to the Tomato and Pesto Grilled Cheese Panini (see recipe in this chapter), so now all you need is a cozy blanket and an excuse to stay home.

SERVES 10

¼ cup olive oil

2 medium yellow onions, peeled and diced

1 bulb garlic, minced

8 large tomatoes, cored and cut into wedges

8 cups vegetable stock

¼ bunch fresh basil, sliced

½ bunch fresh parsley, chopped

¼ recipe Basic Pasta (see sidebar), unformed and uncooked

4 cups cooking oil

½ cup Parmesan cheese curls

1 tablespoon capers, rinsed

1 teaspoon ground black pepper

1. In a large stockpot over medium heat, heat olive oil about 3 minutes. Add onions and sauté about 2 minutes. Add garlic and sauté 2 minutes. Add tomatoes. Reduce heat to low and add vegetable stock. Simmer 1½ hours uncovered.

2. Add basil and parsley and simmer 30 minutes uncovered.
3. While the soup simmers, prepare the fried pasta: Roll out the dough on a floured surface and form as desired. (A spaghetti noodle works well and makes an interesting garnish.) The pasta doesn't need to be cooked unless it has dried. If it has dried, it should be cooked al dente and then drained.
4. In a large, deep pan over medium-high heat, heat 4 cups oil. Fry pasta until lightly golden brown.
5. Serve the soup in individual bowls with clusters of fried pasta. Sprinkle each serving with Parmesan curls, capers, and pepper.

○ ○ ○ ○ **BASIC PASTA** ○ ○ ○ ○

To make your own pasta, you need 3 cups durum wheat (semolina) flour, 1/8 teaspoon iodized salt, 3 large eggs, 1/4 cup olive oil, and 1/4 cup water (room temperature). Sift together the flour and salt into a large mixing bowl. Whisk the eggs in a small bowl. Mix the olive oil and water into the eggs. Make a well in the center of the flour and pour in the egg mixture. Mix together the wet and dry ingredients by hand or in a mixer until the dough forms a ball. Wrap the dough in plastic wrap and let it rest in the refrigerator at least 1 hour. Allow the dough to return to room temperature. Roll out the dough on a floured surface, then form or shape the pasta as desired. Serves 10.

SUMMER VEGETABLE SLAW

Cool breeze, hot sun, and the smell of a charcoal grill bring back fond memories of summer. And if you live in the northern hemisphere, then picnic season is also birthday season for you, Cancer! This vibrant Summer Vegetable Slaw is just the thing to make any meal feel like a celebration, whether you're bringing it to the barbecue or prepping it as a side to enjoy from your own kitchen table. It's brightened with apple cider vinegar and sweetened with a smidge of sugar. Let your tastes lead when it comes to selecting your vegetables. Freshness and deliciousness are the only goals you have in mind, thoughtful Cancer!

SERVES 8

- 1 small head napa cabbage or regular green cabbage (about 1 pound), quartered, cored, and sliced as thinly as possible
- 2 medium carrots, peeled and julienned
- ¼ pound snow peas, julienned
- 1 medium red bell pepper, seeded and julienned
- 1 medium green bell pepper, seeded and julienned
- 1 medium yellow bell pepper, seeded and julienned
- 12 green beans, julienned
- 1 small red onion, peeled and julienned
- 2 medium ears fresh sweet corn, shucked and kernels cut from cobs
- ½ teaspoon granulated sugar
- ¼ cup apple cider vinegar
- 1 tablespoon peanut oil (or vegetable oil)
- ⅛ teaspoon celery seeds
- ⅛ teaspoon salt
- ⅛ teaspoon ground black pepper

In a large bowl, combine all vegetables. Dress with sugar, vinegar, oil, celery seeds, salt, and pepper to taste. Allow to sit at least 10 minutes before serving.

∘∘∘∘ GO WITH YOUR GUT ∘∘∘∘

Your gut never steers you wrong, intuitive Cancer, but now science is beginning to explain why. We keep learning more about the vagus nerve and its relationship to gut health. Eating foods rich in soluble fiber, like cabbage, not only improves digestion but has been shown to reduce inflammation and improve overall mood. All the more reason to eat your slaw!

TARRAGON-ROASTED CHICKEN

Every homebody Cancer has fond memories of delicious aromas emanating from the kitchen and making their way around the house at dinnertime—it makes the home feel so cozy! Achieve those heartwarming home vibes with this Tarragon-Roasted Chicken. Nothing says "comfort food" like a slow-roasted chicken, something Cancer will appreciate serving their family and friends at dinner.

SERVES 8

1 (7-pound) chicken
3 tablespoons olive oil
½ cup loosely packed tarragon, divided
2 tablespoons coarse sea salt

1 tablespoon coarsely ground black pepper
1 tablespoon herbes de Provence

1. Preheat oven to 325°F.
2. Place chicken in a roasting pan. Rub with olive oil. Place half of the tarragon in the chicken cavity.
3. In a small bowl, stir together salt, pepper, remaining tarragon, and herbes de Provence. Rub the mixture onto the skin of chicken.
4. Roast 2 hours, then turn oven temperature up to 350°F.
5. Continue to roast 30 minutes or until chicken is fully cooked. Allow to sit 10 minutes before carving.

∘ ∘ ∘ ∘ **SENSORY SKILLS** ∘ ∘ ∘ ∘

Intuitive Cancers often have an expert sense of smell, which lends to their uncanny ability to judge when food is finished cooking according to scent alone. In fact, Cancers don't even bother setting a timer with familiar dishes. This skill can be attributed to Cancer's impeccable memory. Out of all five senses, scent is most closely linked to memory.

CREAMY MACARONI AND CHEESE WITH SWISS CHARD

Every Cancer has a special place in their heart for mac and cheese—especially baked mac and cheese. Crispy on top and gooey in the middle, this nostalgic recipe includes calcium-rich Swiss chard, so whether you're cooking for yourself or the whole family, you can be sure everyone gets their vegetables. If you have a sensitive stomach, as many Cancer crabs do, feel free to omit the spices in this dish and use oregano or basil instead. Either way, the stars foresee ultimate tummy satisfaction in your future!

SERVES 8

3 tablespoons unsalted butter
3 tablespoons all-purpose flour
½ teaspoon ground cayenne
½ teaspoon paprika
½ teaspoon chipotle flakes
2 cups milk

1 cup shredded sharp Cheddar cheese
1 cup shredded fontina cheese
1 bunch Swiss chard, chopped
1 pound small pasta, cooked and
  drained

1. Preheat oven to 350°F. Lightly grease a 2-quart casserole dish.
2. In a medium pan, melt butter over medium heat. Add flour along with spices and stir until smooth.
3. Add milk and whisk together until slightly thickened, about 5–8 minutes.
4. Whisk in cheeses. Stir in Swiss chard.
5. Pour pasta into casserole dish. Pour the cheese mixture over pasta and stir to evenly distribute.
6. Bake covered about 15 minutes, then uncover and cook until hot and bubbly, about 10–15 additional minutes. Serve.

DILL YOGURT POTATO SALAD

Summer picnics are something every nostalgic Cancer looks forward to. And what's a picnic without potato salad? This recipe offers a fresh take on one of Cancer's summertime favorites with the addition of Greek yogurt—which supplies not only the creamy dressing to this salad but also a healthy dose of probiotics to satisfy your stomach on multidimensional levels. Lemon zest and dill bring bright flavors to this dish, while celery adds the perfect crunch. You're taking potato salad to new heights that everyone at the cookout will appreciate, whimsical Cancer, so fire up the grill and bring this dish along!

SERVES 8

2 pounds whole baby red-skin potatoes
1 medium onion, peeled and diced
1 medium shallot, peeled and minced
4 large red radishes, diced
⅓ cup diced cucumber
2 medium stalks celery, diced

¾ cup chopped fresh dill
1¼ cups plain Greek yogurt
¼ cup lemon juice
2 tablespoons lemon zest
½ teaspoon sea salt
½ teaspoon ground white pepper

1. In a medium bowl, combine potatoes, onion, shallot, radishes, cucumber, and celery. Set aside.
2. In a small bowl, stir together dill, yogurt, lemon juice, lemon zest, salt, and pepper. Pour over the potato mixture and stir to evenly coat.
3. Refrigerate 2 hours prior to serving.

STUFFED SHELLS

Celestial Cancer crabs always find themselves at home in a shell, which is why you're making stuffed shells! You adore a cheesy baked shell covered in sweet marinara sauce, thoughtful Cancer, but so does everyone else! Show your loved ones you care by bringing this special homemade treat to the next party.

SERVES 10

PASTA

2 cups spelt flour
1 cup all-purpose flour
1/8 teaspoon iodized salt
3 large eggs
1 large egg white
1/4 cup olive oil
1 tablespoon water

FILLING

1 cup mascarpone cheese
1/2 cup Gorgonzola cheese
3 large eggs
1 teaspoon red pepper flakes
1/2 bunch fresh basil, chopped
4 cups pasta sauce of your choice, divided

1. In a large mixing bowl, sift together spelt flour, all-purpose flour, and salt.
2. In a small bowl, whisk together eggs and egg white. Mix olive oil and water into eggs.
3. Make a well in the center of the flour mixture and pour in the egg mixture. Mix together the wet and dry ingredients by hand or in a mixer with a dough hook until the dough forms a ball. Wrap the dough in plastic wrap and let it rest in the refrigerator at least 1 hour or up to 1 day.
4. Preheat oven to 350°F. Allow the dough to return to room temperature.
5. In a large bowl, mix together mascarpone, Gorgonzola, eggs, red pepper flakes, and basil.
6. Ladle 1/2 cup sauce into a large baking pan to coat the bottom of the pan.
7. Roll out dough on a floured surface into a sheet about 1/2" thick. Cut into 4" ovals.
8. Place 2 heaping tablespoons of the cheese mixture in the center of each oval. Fold up two edges and pinch the ends together to form shells. Place in the pan. Ladle remaining sauce over the top of the shells.
9. Cover and bake 20 minutes. Uncover and bake 5 more minutes until lightly browned and bubbling. Serve.

APPLE PIE

Apple Pie is a quintessential symbol of Americana—right there with baseball, drive-ins, and rock 'n' roll. Fresh-baked Apple Pie is also a beloved staple on doting Cancer's dinner table. Cancers adore the sweet, spiced apples baked into the ultimate phyllo pie crust. This recipe features a pie crust layered with those favorite cinnamon spices and ground almonds for an extra dose of sweetness and texture. Vanilla ice cream is always an optional topping, dear Cancer.

SERVES 8

7 medium Granny Smith apples
2 tablespoons lemon juice
½ cup brown sugar
⅓ cup orange juice
¼ cup all-purpose flour
¼ teaspoon salt
1 teaspoon ground cinnamon
¼ teaspoon ground nutmeg

⅛ teaspoon cardamom
10 (9" × 14") sheets frozen phyllo
   dough, thawed
3 tablespoons butter, melted, divided
2 tablespoons honey
5 tablespoons ground almonds, divided
5 tablespoons granulated sugar,
   divided

1. Preheat oven to 375°F. Spray a 9" pie pan with butter-flavored nonstick cooking spray and set aside.
2. Peel, core, and slice apples ½" thick, sprinkling with lemon juice as you work.
3. In a large saucepan over medium heat, combine apples, brown sugar, orange juice, flour, salt, cinnamon, nutmeg, and cardamom. Bring to a simmer, then reduce heat to low and simmer until apples are crisp-tender, about 8–10 minutes. Remove from heat and set aside.

4. Place one sheet of phyllo dough on a clean work surface. In a small bowl, combine 2 tablespoons butter and honey and mix well. Brush the butter mixture over dough and sprinkle with 1 tablespoon almonds and 1 tablespoon granulated sugar. Top with another layer of dough. Repeat this process until you have five stacks of dough, each two layers thick.

5. Place dough in prepared pan, starting from just below the lip of the pan, letting dough fall across the bottom and over the other edge. Spray with butter-flavored nonstick cooking spray and layer another stack on top, turning it slightly so about 1/3 of the pie plate is covered. Continue in this manner until the pan is covered with dough stacks.

6. Spoon in the apple filling. Gently pull the overhanging edges of phyllo dough over the filling, pleating to fit. Brush with remaining 1 tablespoon butter.

7. Bake 23–30 minutes or until dough is golden brown and crisp and apples are bubbling and tender. Let cool 1 hour, then serve.

○ ○ ○ ○ **SET THE MOOD WITH A TUNE** ○ ○ ○ ○

Sentimental Cancers often have an impressive music collection filled with a variety of genres to suit their vast pantheon of moods. Music speaks to this celestial crab's soul in a deep way, so don't be surprised to learn that they've made a playlist for every occasion—including tonight's dinner party.

SLOW COOKER CIDER

Nurturing Cancers crave a beverage that brings people together. Enter this Slow Cooker Cider—a boozy beverage spiked with the mellow spices of cinnamon and clove. Cancers can't resist a mulled apple cider, so you'll especially love this hands-free recipe with a twist. This warm concoction simmers on low, sending delicious aromas throughout your home and signaling to everyone to grab a mug and fill it up! It doesn't get cozier than this, Cancer. There's nothing Cancer loves more than feeding their loved ones, and now you can get them tipsy too! What fun!

SERVES 10

4 (12-ounce) bottles hard apple (or pear) cider
8 ounces pear vodka
4 ounces brown sugar
2 cups cranberry juice

2 cinnamon sticks
Rind of 1 medium orange studded with whole cloves
Orange slices, for garnish

Put all the ingredients except orange slices in a large slow cooker set on low for 4 hours. Serve warm, garnished with orange slices.

CLASSIC CHOCOLATE CHIP COOKIES

Chocolate chip cookies are a favorite sweet snack of sentimental Cancerians. They're a timeless comfort food with multiple variations, and this recipe offers you a softer, fluffier cookie using whole-wheat flour and room-temperature butter. Celestial crustaceans always cook intuitively, so let your mood guide you to keep it classic with granulated sugar, or use brown sugar for a more full-bodied buttery flavor. Cancers will enjoy these cookies in between meals on a lazy Sunday or as an after-school pick-me-up. You always know how to make us feel the love, nurturing Cancer!

YIELDS 2 DOZEN COOKIES

6 tablespoons unsalted butter, at room temperature
¾ cup granulated sugar
1 large egg, at room temperature
1 teaspoon vanilla extract

1 cup white whole-wheat flour
⅓ cup all-purpose flour
½ teaspoon baking powder
¼ teaspoon salt
6 ounces dark chocolate chips

1. Preheat oven to 350°F. Line two cookie sheets with parchment paper.
2. In a large bowl, cream together butter and sugar.
3. Beat in egg and vanilla.
4. In a medium bowl, whisk together the flours, baking powder, and salt. Add to the butter mixture and mix until well combined. Fold in chocolate chips.
5. Place tablespoons of dough 2" apart on prepared cookie sheets. Bake 12 minutes or until the tops of the cookies are mostly set and the bottoms are golden. Carefully remove to a wire rack and cool completely.

Leo:
The Luminous Chef

Lovable Leo, you're the lion of the zodiac, which means you have a certain regalness about you. You know you're awesome, and sometimes these facts need to be known. Roar! As the fixed fire sign of the zodiac, your fire is contained, which lends to your inherent warmth and gravitas. Leo is ruled by the life-sustaining Sun in the center of the solar system, so it's no wonder these expressive felines are mighty comfortable in the spotlight! Glowing Leos often boast a distinguishing physical feature, be it their mane, signature style, or even their vivacious laugh. These extravagant lions are unafraid to make a statement!

Leo rules the heart—which is evident by their marked generosity, affection, and dramatic gestures. Celestial lions are proud of who they are, but they've got an even bigger love for the others in their pride, often hoisting their loved ones high up onto a pedestal. These cosmic kittens are indeed playful. Your Leo pals are always up for a good time, and they love playing host! Entertainers by nature, Leos captivate their guests with a full menu of class-act dishes to be enjoyed around lively dinner conversation. But their favorite purring indulgence is lounging in the lion's den together after the meal. And if you're invited, you can certainly be proud to be a part of this lion's pride. So roam at your own will, Leo, this menu is sure to dazzle with star-studded dishes.

IRISH OATMEAL AND POACHED FRUIT

Lively Leos love an energizing and outstandingly yummy breakfast. Irish oats boast a thick texture and a delicious nutty flavor, and they are guaranteed to keep you full longer than quick oats. As the fixed fire sign of the zodiac, you appreciate a breakfast that energizes you all morning, helping you maintain your steady vibrancy. Costarring fresh fruit and sweet honey, this recipe makes enough for two or three people, so go ahead and double the measurements if the whole family is hungry.

SERVES 4

1 medium fresh peach, pitted and chopped
½ cup raisins
1 medium tart apple, cored and chopped
½ cup water

3 tablespoons honey
½ teaspoon salt
2 cups Irish or Scottish oatmeal
1½ cups skim milk
1½ cups low-fat yogurt
1 cup toasted walnuts

1. In a medium saucepan, mix peach, raisins, and apple with water, honey, and salt. Bring to a boil and remove from heat. Set aside.
2. In a separate medium saucepan, mix oatmeal and milk with yogurt. Cook according to package directions.
3. Mix the cooked fruit mixture into the oatmeal and cook another 2–3 minutes. Serve hot, sprinkled with walnuts.

○ ○ ○ ○ **HEART HEALTHY** ○ ○ ○ ○

Ruled by the life-giving Sun, luminous Leos are typically blessed with resilient immune systems. In the body, Leo rules the heart. Leos must care for their heart in two ways: Eat heart-healthy foods like oatmeal, and secondly, follow your passions!

TOMATO AND GOAT CHEESE BREAKFAST CASSEROLE

Generous Leos love waking up early so they can surprise their loved ones with breakfast. And good thing, too, because this spectacular casserole has a long bake time on it. Fresh oregano gives a unique savory flair to your breakfast, and it expertly elevates the flavors of the tomato and goat cheese. Leos love making a statement—so send a strong signal with this beyond-delicious dish. Expressive Leos might like to present this elegant cheesy casserole to friends and family on a Sunday morning, or enjoy it for themselves throughout the week. Leave it to leonine Leo to prepare a unique breakfast that leaves us all wanting more.

SERVES 6

8 large eggs
1 cup whole milk
1 teaspoon salt
1 teaspoon ground black pepper

2 cups halved cherry tomatoes
¼ cup chopped fresh oregano
4 ounces goat cheese, diced

1. In a medium bowl, whisk eggs, milk, salt, and pepper together. Stir in tomatoes, oregano, and goat cheese and mix well.
2. Grease a 4- to 5-quart slow cooker with olive oil.
3. Pour the egg mixture into slow cooker and cook on low 4–6 hours or on high 2–3 hours. The casserole is done when a knife inserted into the center comes out clean. Serve hot.

SPA CUCUMBER SMOOTHIE

Here's a soothing sipper guaranteed to make leonine Leo purr. Leos of the northern hemisphere were born during the hottest of summer days, and similarly, Leo, you, too, can be too hot to handle! Cooling cucumber and hydrating lime are just the thing to quench Leo's thirst. As a fire sign who is prone to dryness, cucumber is excellent for the skin and the overall hydration of the body. This smoothie is the perfect soothing drink for someone like you who loves to relax—whether getting a pedicure or lounging at home.

YIELDS 1½ CUPS

2 medium cucumbers, peeled and cut into chunks
Juice of 1 medium lime

½ cup filtered water
3 teaspoons raw honey
1 cup ice

1. Combine the ingredients in a blender and purée until smooth.
2. Serve immediately.

∘ ∘ ∘ ∘ SOME LIKE IT HOT ∘ ∘ ∘ ∘

One thing you'll always get with a Leo is passion. This hot fire sign's reputation for the dramatic is well founded. Sometimes they can get a little feisty, but you will always get the unfiltered truth. Leos should aim to eat foods that are cooling in nature—like cucumbers!

HUMMUS AND TOFU SANDWICHES

Lions need to eat, so lead the way to the kitchen, regal Leo! This time, lunch is a high-protein vegan sandwich, highlighting hummus and thinly sliced tofu. Tofu is packaged in water, so for best results, gently press the tofu slices between paper towels before starting anything else (cutting boards work great here). Tofu takes on the flavor of whatever it surrounds, so there's room to play with seasonings if you're thinking ahead, creative Leo. Overall, fiery Leo will adore the softness of this stellar sandwich, the refreshing crunch from the vegetables, and the subtle blend of herbs. Looks like the stars have smiled upon you once again, sunny Leo!

SERVES 2

½ cup classic hummus
4 slices whole-grain bread
1 medium seedless cucumber, sliced
1 small red onion, peeled and sliced

2 tablespoons minced fresh oregano
4 ounces firm tofu, cut into slices
1 tablespoon dill mustard

1. Divide hummus between two slices of bread. Top with cucumber, onion, oregano, and tofu.
2. Spread mustard on remaining slices of bread. Top the sandwiches. Serve.

∘ ∘ ∘ ∘ IT'S ALWAYS TIME TO TALK! ∘ ∘ ∘ ∘

Leos love to talk, so why not whip up these sandwiches and invite a friend over to nosh and have some fun? Get-togethers don't always have to revolve around dinnertime meals; have a lunch party with these refreshing and healthy sandwiches and share some quality time with a friend!

BANH MI
(Vietnamese Sandwich)

Leo starlets often have exclusive tastes, so here's your VIP ticket: the one-of-a-kind Banh Mi. Lively Leos will adore the spectacular cast of flavors harmonizing in this vivacious Vietnamese sandwich. You'll need the softest baguettes you can find, premium grilled pork, and crunchy vegetables. You'll need to make the pickled vegetables at least an hour ahead of time, but if you make a big batch, they can keep in the refrigerator up to 3 weeks. In that case, the stars foresee an abundance of showstopping sandwiches in your future, Leo!

SERVES 4

1 (24") baguette cut into 4 pieces, or
    4 (6") Vietnamese baguettes
¼ cup Japanese mayonnaise
8 slices ham
2 cups sliced grilled pork

1 medium cucumber, peeled and thinly
    sliced lengthwise
8 large cilantro sprigs
1 medium jalapeño, thinly sliced
½ cup Đo Chua (see sidebar)

1. Preheat oven to 350°F.
2. Place baguettes on a baking sheet and bake 5 minutes, or until crispy. Split baguettes lengthwise, making sure not to cut all the way through.
3. Spread each baguette with mayonnaise, then layer in ham, grilled pork, cucumber, cilantro, jalapeño, and Đo Chua. Slice each sandwich in half and serve.

◦ ◦ ◦ ◦ ĐO CHUA ◦ ◦ ◦ ◦
(Vietnamese Pickled Carrots and Daikon)

These pickled vegetables are quick to make and are ready to eat in an hour, but they can also last for 3 weeks if kept refrigerated. This recipe will make 3 cups.
Take ½ pound carrots (peeled and julienned), ½ pound daikon radish (peeled and julienned), 3 tablespoons granulated sugar, 1 teaspoon salt, 1 cup vinegar, and 1 cup warm water. Place carrots and daikon into a large sterile glass canning jar. Set aside. In a medium glass bowl, combine the sugar, salt, vinegar, and water. Mix until dissolved. Pour the mixture over the vegetables until the jar is full. Cover with a lid and refrigerate 1 hour before serving.

BLACKBERRY FLAX MUFFINS

These heart-healthy muffins are the perfect snack for passionate Leos. Blackberries give these muffins a subtle pop of violet color, making them even more fun to eat. Leos can appreciate flaxseed, a superfood that benefits digestive, brain, and heart functions while adding a nutty dimension to these stellar muffins. Leo will also enjoy sharing these tasty muffins with their friends, family, or even coworkers.
Leave it to you to share the love, Leo!

YIELDS 12 MUFFINS

1½ cups white whole-wheat flour
¼ cup flaxseed meal
1 teaspoon baking powder
1 teaspoon baking soda
½ teaspoon ground ginger

½ cup dark brown sugar
½ cup buttermilk
½ cup canola oil
1 teaspoon vanilla extract
1¾ cups fresh blackberries

1. Preheat oven to 350°F. Line or grease and flour twelve wells in a muffin tin.
2. In a medium bowl, whisk together flour, flaxseed meal, baking powder, baking soda, ginger, and brown sugar.
3. In a small bowl, whisk together buttermilk, oil, and vanilla until well combined. Pour into the dry ingredients and stir until just mixed. Fold in blackberries.
4. Evenly divide the batter among the wells in prepared muffin tin. Bake 20 minutes or until a toothpick inserted in the center of the center muffin comes out clean.

CHICKEN SATAY WITH PEANUT SAUCE

Okay, fiery Leo, here's a dish that appeals to your spicy side. And we must warn you that this appetizer is so delicious that there could be a fight over the last piece. A little drama doesn't scare you, playful Leo, but plan on making plenty to avoid such scenarios.

SERVES 8

CHICKEN

2 cloves garlic, minced

1 teaspoon minced ginger

2 tablespoons soy sauce

1 teaspoon sesame oil

¼ teaspoon red pepper flakes

4 tablespoons vegetable oil, divided

1 pound boneless, skinless chicken breast, cut into 1" cubes

2 medium scallions, sliced and ends trimmed

2 tablespoons crushed roasted peanuts

PEANUT SAUCE

1 cup smooth peanut butter

1 tablespoon grated ginger

2 teaspoons sesame oil

1 tablespoon soy sauce

2 cloves garlic, minced

1 teaspoon red pepper flakes

2 tablespoons rice vinegar

¼ teaspoon kosher salt

¼ cup peanut oil

---

1. In a large bowl, whisk together garlic, ginger, soy sauce, sesame oil, pepper flakes, and 2 tablespoons oil. Add chicken and toss to coat well. Refrigerate 30 minutes.

2. Meanwhile, make the peanut sauce: In a blender, add peanut butter, ginger, sesame oil, soy sauce, garlic, red pepper flakes, rice vinegar, and salt. Blend until combined. On the lowest setting, stream in peanut oil until completely emulsified, approximately 2–3 minutes.

3. Heat remaining vegetable oil in a wok over medium-high heat. Add chicken with the marinade liquid (be careful of splattering). Stir-fry 3–4 minutes until chicken is cooked through.

4. Place chicken on a plate and drizzle the cooking liquids over the top. Top chicken with scallions and peanuts. Serve with peanut sauce.

FARRO WITH RAINBOW CHARD

Farro is a heart-healthy grain you'll appreciate, lovable Leo! If you haven't yet sampled this outstanding ancient grain, now's your chance. This powerful wheat berry is like short-grain brown rice, but with a nuttier flavor and a chewier texture. Glamorous Leos will feel like they are getting the special treatment with this dish—overflowing with antioxidants, minerals, and, yes, even protein. Rainbow chard and carrots bring gorgeous color to the plate that showy Leos will adore. Pair with the Pistachio-Crusted Halibut (see recipe in this chapter) for a meal that's over-the-top in color and flavor. Just brace yourself for the standing ovation, dramatic Leo!

--- SERVES 4 ---

4 cups water
1 cup farro
1 medium shallot, peeled and chopped
1 medium carrot, peeled and diced
1 medium stalk celery, diced
2 cloves garlic, minced

2 tablespoons olive oil
¼ cup chopped fresh Italian parsley
1 bunch rainbow chard, roughly chopped
1½ tablespoons tarragon vinegar

1. In a medium saucepan over high heat, bring water and farro to a boil. Reduce heat to low and simmer until tender, stirring occasionally, about 25 minutes. Drain.
2. Meanwhile, in a medium skillet over medium heat, sauté shallot, carrot, celery, and garlic in olive oil until shallots are transparent, about 5–7 minutes. Add parsley and chard and sauté until they start to wilt, about 2–3 minutes. Remove from heat. Stir in farro.
3. Drizzle with vinegar. Serve hot or at room temperature.

PUMPKIN ALE SOUP

Puréed pumpkin gives this soup a delightful golden hue that every luminous Leo will appreciate. Finally, a dish as sunny as you! Even though this soup is best enjoyed warm, fire signs can benefit from the cooling and grounding qualities pumpkin provides. This naturally creamy soup is complemented superbly with thyme and beer! Leo, you're one of the party animals of the zodiac, so you'll delight in dumping a bottle of brew into this soup. A word of caution here, though: Avoid hoppy pale ales or you'll end up with a not-so-palatable bitter astringent taste. But if pumpkin beer is in season, you are in luck, brilliant Leo!

--- **SERVES 6** ---

2 (15-ounce) cans pumpkin purée
¼ cup diced onion
2 cloves garlic, minced
2 teaspoons salt

1 teaspoon ground black pepper
¼ teaspoon dried thyme
5 cups vegetable broth
1 (12-ounce) bottle pale ale beer

1. In a 4-quart slow cooker, add pumpkin purée, onion, garlic, salt, pepper, thyme, and vegetable broth. Stir well. Cover and cook over low heat 4 hours.
2. Allow the soup to cool slightly, then process in a blender or with an immersion blender until smooth.
3. Pour the soup back into slow cooker, add beer, and cook 1 hour over low heat.
4. Stir and serve.

GREEN BEAN SALAD WITH ORANGE VINAIGRETTE

Leos adore a showstopping dish. This easy, anytime salad is suitable any day of the week, but it's also fancy enough to be served with a holiday meal. Green beans are the star of this show, supported by the sunny orange and vivacious cherries. If you don't have a zester, a vegetable peeler will suffice (just be sure to avoid the white pith). Heartfelt Leo will purr at this salad's perfect balance of color, texture, and tantalizing taste. This sunny salad can be enjoyed warm or cold, but since you are a natural leader, Leo, we'll trust you to call the shots on this one!

SERVES 8

2 pounds French green beans (haricots verts), steamed
⅓ cup toasted hazelnuts
¼ cup dried tart cherries
1 small onion, peeled and minced

2 tablespoons extra-virgin olive oil
3 tablespoons white wine vinegar
3 tablespoons fresh orange juice
1 tablespoon orange zest
½ teaspoon Dijon mustard

1. In a large bowl, toss together green beans, hazelnuts, and cherries. Set aside.
2. In a small bowl, whisk together onion, oil, vinegar, orange juice, orange zest, and mustard until well combined. Drizzle over the green bean mixture and toss again. Serve warm or cold.

PISTACHIO-CRUSTED HALIBUT

Radiant Leos will eagerly pounce on this exquisite seafood fare. Costarring the zests of three vibrant citrus fruits, milky-green pistachios, and bold-hued parsley, the crust on this halibut is as visually stunning as it is delicious! For how glamorous this dish may be, it's surprisingly easy to make. Pair with the Farro with Rainbow Chard side dish (see recipe in this chapter), and you'll be feeling fierce up in this kitchen!

SERVES 4

½ cup roughly chopped shelled unsalted pistachios
2 teaspoons grated lemon zest
1 teaspoon grated lime zest
2 teaspoons grated orange zest
4 teaspoons chopped fresh parsley
1 cup bread crumbs
¼ cup extra-virgin olive oil
4 (6-ounce) halibut fillets, skins removed
1½ teaspoons salt
½ teaspoon ground black pepper
4 teaspoons Dijon mustard

1. Preheat oven to 400°F. Line a baking sheet with parchment paper.
2. In a food processor, pulse pistachios, zests, parsley, and bread crumbs to combine the ingredients. With the processor running, add oil until well incorporated.
3. Rinse fish and pat dry with a paper towel. Season fish with salt and pepper.
4. Brush the tops of fish with mustard. Divide the pistachio mixture evenly and place some on the top of each fish. Press down on the mixture to help the crust adhere.
5. Carefully place crusted fish on prepared baking sheet. Bake 20 minutes or until crust is golden brown.
6. Let cool 5 minutes, and serve immediately.

CHICKPEAS IN POTATO AND ONION CURRY

Laid-back Leos will appreciate the mellow warmth of the spices highlighted in this dish. Though Indian cuisine can really bring the heat, this recipe keeps the fire contained—just like you know how to do. Ruled by the Sun, your warmth is steady and captivating to others. And fortunately for you, lucky Leo, this delicious Chickpeas in Potato and Onion Curry has the same effect! It's enjoyable as is, over rice, or paired with garlic naan. Whether you're cooking for the whole family or just having a lazy week (we know how you lions and lionesses love to lounge), go ahead and double your recipe to enjoy leftovers later.

SERVES 4

2 cups chopped (1") onions
3 tablespoons olive oil, divided
1½ cups cubed (1") potatoes
1 (14-ounce) can coconut milk
1 (15-ounce) can chickpeas, drained
    and rinsed
5 cloves garlic

1 teaspoon kosher salt
1½ teaspoons ground coriander
½ teaspoon ground turmeric
1 teaspoon chili powder
1 teaspoon ground cumin
Juice of ½ medium lemon

1. In a medium skillet over high heat, cook onions in 1 tablespoon oil until lightly browned, about 5 minutes.
2. Add potatoes and coconut milk; cover and cook until potatoes are tender, about 20 minutes; add chickpeas.
3. In a food processor, combine garlic, salt, coriander, turmeric, chili powder, and cumin; process until it becomes a paste, scraping down sides as needed.
4. Heat remaining oil in a small skillet over medium heat and fry the garlic mixture 1 minute, allowing it to become fragrant and slightly browned. Add the garlic mixture to the chickpea skillet. Simmer 2–3 minutes; season with lemon juice. Serve.

TRADITIONAL LASAGNA

Leos are generous hosts who aim to impress their guests—which is why you want to serve a dish that everyone can get excited about, like lasagna! Characterized by its lovable layers of cheese, sauce, and flavorful meats, this is one foodie favorite guaranteed to be a hit at your next party. Your guests won't be able to resist the cheesy allure of this baked deep dish, and neither will you, loyal Leo. Whether you're going for comfort food at a casual family gathering or an evening dinner party with your friends, lasagna is a popular dish that you'll be proud to see your loved ones devour.

SERVES 10

1 (1-pound) box lasagna noodles
8 cups tomato sauce of choice
1 pound ground beef, cooked
1 pound sweet Italian sausage, cooked
¾ cup ricotta cheese

1 cup shredded mozzarella cheese
¼ cup fresh-grated Parmesan cheese
3 sprigs fresh basil, chopped
3 sprigs fresh oregano, chopped
½ teaspoon ground black pepper

1. Preheat oven to 350°F.
2. Bring a large pot of water to a slow boil, add pasta, and cook until al dente, about 10 minutes. Shock in bowl of ice water to stop cooking.
3. Spoon a thin layer of tomato sauce into the bottom of a large baking pan. Layer pasta sheets over the sauce, then top with a layer of beef, sausage, cheeses, basil, oregano, and pepper. Ladle more sauce over the top. Repeat layering until the pan is almost full, finishing with a top layer of pasta, sauce, and cheeses.
4. Cover and bake 45 minutes. Uncover and bake 15 minutes or until lightly browned and bubbling.
5. Remove from oven and let stand 5–10 minutes before serving.

CHEESE-STUFFED BIFTEKI

Out of all the fire signs, Leo is the natural grill master. And everyone would really appreciate it if you offered your outstanding grill skills to make us some juicy burgers. Bifteki is simply a Greek-style hamburger stuffed with cheese. This recipe uses Graviera, a Greek cheese, but if you can't find Graviera, Muenster cheese is another tasty option for luminous Leos. Once your burgers are grilled to perfection, layer on a bun as you would with any other burger, and get ready for everyone to sing your praises.

SERVES 6

2 pounds ground beef
2 medium onions, peeled and grated
3 slices bread, soaked in water, hand-squeezed, and crumbled
1 tablespoon minced garlic
1 teaspoon dried oregano
1 teaspoon chopped fresh parsley
¼ teaspoon ground allspice
2 tablespoons salt
1 teaspoon ground black pepper
6 (1") cubes Graviera cheese
3 tablespoons vegetable oil

1. In a large bowl, combine all the ingredients except cheese and oil and mix thoroughly.
2. Using your hands, form twelve (4" × ½") patties with the ground beef mixture. Place patties on a tray, cover with plastic wrap, and refrigerate 4 hours or overnight.
3. Allow patties to come to room temperature before grilling.
4. Take a piece of cheese and place it on the middle of a patty. Place another patty on top and press together to form one burger. Using your fingers, pinch the entire perimeter of the burger to seal.
5. Preheat a gas or charcoal grill to medium-high. Brush grill surface to make sure it is thoroughly clean. When grill is ready, dip a clean tea towel in vegetable oil and wipe the grill surface with oil. Place burgers on grill and cook 5 minutes per side.
6. Allow burgers to rest 5 minutes before serving.

KEY LIME BARS

Lively Leos know how to party. Keep the crowd roaring with a late-night sweet treat like these Key Lime Bars. Leo cannot pass up the distinctive taste of key lime—exquisitely fluffy and irresistibly tangy, especially in dessert form. The graham cracker crust takes this treat to the next level, adding necessary elements of texture and salt. It's basically a bite-sized margarita, Leo, so put on your favorite Hawaiian shirt (or dress) and serve up these tasty squares with gusto! Another thing you'll appreciate? These beautiful green bites will be as eye-catching as you are, fashionable Leo!

SERVES 12

2 cups graham cracker crumbs
¼ cup unsalted butter, melted and cooled slightly
4 large eggs, at room temperature
1¾ cups granulated sugar

¾ cup freshly squeezed key lime juice
¾ cup all-purpose flour
2 tablespoons key lime zest, divided
5 key limes, sliced into thin slices

1. Preheat oven to 350°F.
2. In a small bowl, mix together graham cracker crumbs and butter with a fork. Press into the bottom of an 8" × 8" baking pan. Bake 5 minutes. Set aside.
3. Meanwhile, in a medium bowl, whisk together eggs, sugar, key lime juice, flour, and 1½ tablespoons zest. Pour over the graham cracker crust.
4. Return pan to oven and bake 35 minutes or until the bars are fully set. Cool completely before slicing. Sprinkle with remaining lime zest and top each with a lime slice and serve.

ORANGE AND LEMON OLIVE OIL CAKE

Here's a cake worthy of parading down the cakewalk, lustrous Leo! Leos seek a cake that is both sumptuous and light for summer celebrations, so look no further than this olive oil Bundt cake. Orange and lemon supply the bright citrus notes to this cake, while a sweet lemony icing lightly drizzles over the iconic Bundt mounds. Who knew dessert could be so...refreshing? Sunny Leos will love pouncing on this tasty summer treat as much as they will love sharing it with their loved ones.

SERVES 12

2½ cups all-purpose flour
1¾ cups granulated sugar
2 teaspoons baking powder
1 teaspoon baking soda
¼ teaspoon salt
⅓ cup orange juice
⅓ cup plus ¼ cup lemon juice, divided

⅓ cup buttermilk
¾ cup light olive oil
2 teaspoons vanilla extract
1 large egg
5 large egg whites
1 cup confectioners' sugar

1. Preheat oven to 325°F. Spray a 12-cup Bundt pan with nonstick baking spray containing flour; set aside.
2. In a large bowl, combine flour, sugar, baking powder, baking soda, and salt and mix well; set aside.
3. In a medium bowl, combine orange juice, ⅓ cup lemon juice, buttermilk, olive oil, vanilla, and egg; beat until combined. Stir into the flour mixture; beat until blended.
4. In a small bowl, beat egg whites until stiff. Fold into the batter until combined.
5. Pour the batter into prepared pan. Bake 40–50 minutes or until cake is dark golden brown and a toothpick inserted in the center comes out clean.
6. In a small bowl, combine confectioners' sugar and ¼ cup lemon juice; mix well. Spoon half over the cake in the pan.
7. Loosen the edges of cake and turn out onto a serving plate. Spoon the remaining confectioners' sugar mixture over the cake; let cool completely.

VESPER

*Luminous Leos never pass up a trendy cocktail. Go with the Vesper!
Elegantly combining gin, vodka, and Lillet Blanc, the Vesper boasts delicate
notes of floral and citrus. But all in all, Leo, there's nothing dainty about this
martini. In fact, this concoction was invented by James Bond, so you know
it's brilliant! Leonine starlets will be charmed by this bold yet sexy cocktail.
"Vesper" means "evening" in Latin, so shake up this sophisticated martini,
Leo, and you'll feel like the brightest star of the evening. You, too,
will feel like an evening star with the sophisticated
Vesper martini, dear Leo.*

SERVES 1

---

3 ounces gin
1 ounce vodka

½ ounce Lillet Blanc
1 lemon twist

---

1. Shake all the liquid ingredients with ice. Strain into a martini glass.
2. Garnish with lemon twist.

Virgo:
The Logical Chef

Analytical, methodical, and incredibly thoughtful, Virgo is represented by the immaculate virgin bearing a sheaf of wheat. No, not all Virgos can be considered virginal by modern standards, but these tidy perfectionists are highly cultivated and geared toward self-mastery. With a penchant for organization and an eye for detail, Virgo will notice nuances others are willing to skip over, which leads to an exquisite quality of their work. These compassionate logicians are natural problem solvers and some of the most thoughtful of friends. Ruled by deft Mercury, Virgos are clever, agile, and crafty, though the devil is in the details for these earthy perfectionists!

Virgos tend to be healthy eaters by nature. They understand that the more optimally the body runs, the more they can accomplish! Virgos like to keep busy. And with the precise balance of detail-mindedness and creativity, these folks tend to do very well for themselves. In fact, Virgos are overrepresented in the world of celebrity chefs, which tells us that these details matter in the kitchen. Favoring simple dishes, these thoughtful intellectuals are willing to take the extra time to elevate a dish from good to excellent. You value simple elegance on a plate, Virgo, so you can look forward to dishes like Honey-Glazed Filet Mignon and Miso Soup!

SPINACH AND RICOTTA MINI QUICHES

Few things are more satisfying to sharp-eyed Virgo than order—and muffin pans are an excellent way to get there! Virgos will take as much pleasure in the uniformity of these perfectly portioned mini quiches as they will the flavor. Ricotta cheese lends a superb creamy and airy texture to these quiches that Virgo will rate "A+!" For ultimate uniformity, top each quiche with a small tomato slice and shredded cheese before baking. Your quiches will keep in the refrigerator for a few days, so if you know you can't eat them fast enough, you can always surprise your family with breakfast. You're thoughtful like that, Virgo.

SERVES 6

10 ounces chopped frozen spinach
2 large eggs
1 cup skim ricotta cheese

1 cup low-fat shredded mozzarella cheese

1. Preheat oven to 350°F. Place cupcake liners in the wells of a twelve-cup muffin tin.
2. Place spinach in a medium microwave-safe bowl and heat according to package directions until soft and warm.
3. In a medium bowl, whip eggs. Add spinach and blend together. Fold in the ricotta and mozzarella cheeses.
4. Fill each muffin cup with the egg and spinach mixture, about ½" per cup. Bake 30–35 minutes. Serve.

FIG, APRICOT, AND ALMOND GRANOLA

Thoughtful Virgo understands that homemade is always the best way to go, especially when it comes to honey-spiced granola. This recipe features cardamom, one of the mellowest of spices around. Included in chai tea blends, cardamom is valued for its ability to soothe digestive ailments and stop the flu in its tracks—all the more reason to start your morning with homemade granola! Serve over Greek yogurt and slices of fresh strawberries for an out-of-this-world breakfast that meets your high standards of deliciousness, idyllic Virgo!

SERVES 16

⅓ cup vegetable oil
⅓ cup honey
2 tablespoons granulated sugar
1 teaspoon vanilla extract
4 cups old-fashioned oats
1¼ cups sliced almonds

½ cup chopped dried apricots
½ cup chopped dried figs
½ cup packed brown sugar
½ teaspoon salt
½ teaspoon ground cardamom

1. Preheat oven to 300°F. Lightly spray two large baking sheets with nonstick vegetable oil spray.
2. In a small saucepan over medium heat, add oil, honey, granulated sugar, and vanilla. Cook 5 minutes or until sugar is dissolved. Remove pan from heat and let it cool 2 minutes.
3. In a large bowl, combine oats, almonds, apricots, figs, brown sugar, salt, and cardamom. Mix with your hands to combine.
4. Pour the honey mixture over the oat mixture. Using your hands (if it is too hot, use a wooden spoon), toss the ingredients together to make sure everything is well coated. Spread granola evenly over two baking sheets. Bake 30 minutes, stirring every 10 minutes.
5. Let granola cool completely on the baking sheets, then break it up into pieces. Store in an airtight container up to 3 weeks.

APRICOT ALMOND DELIGHT SMOOTHIES

Here's a high-protein smoothie that's sure to pique your curiosity, analytical Virgo. How can something possibly taste this good and still be healthy for you? Don't even try to figure this one out, Virgo. Few things in this world are more delicious than apricot nectar. Energizing almonds make this smoothie a perfect midmorning sipper to help you keep the ball rolling, while high-protein yogurt keeps you full until your next meal. As you like it, practical Virgo, this one is fairly straightforward: Just sip and enjoy!

SERVES 2

1½ cups fresh apricot nectar
1 cup vanilla low-fat yogurt
2 tablespoons almond butter

1 tablespoon raw honey
1 cup ice

1. Combine all the ingredients in a blender and process until smooth.
2. Serve immediately.

◦ ◦ ◦ ◦ QUICK ON YOUR TOES ◦ ◦ ◦ ◦

As the mutable earth sign, Virgo is an agile problem solver. Quick-thinking, intelligent, and practical, these thoughtful logicians are not intimidated by a roadblock. They will always find a way around it. So if they go to make this smoothie and have no almond butter on hand, they won't panic or fret. They'll simply soak a handful of almonds, add ⅛ teaspoon salt, and blend away!

HOMEMADE BEAN AND VEGETABLE BURGERS

Don't be too skeptical here, Virgo; these veggie burgers are homemade! Slightly spicy and high in protein, these flavorful patties will outdo any frozen ones around. Who knew veggie burgers were so easy to make? Detail-oriented Virgos are excellent strategists, which is why you'll appreciate the culinary crossovers here. You might preemptively set aside one of the Roasted Yukon Gold Potatoes (see recipe in this chapter) for this recipe, while your California Garden Salad with Avocado and Sprouts fixings (see recipe in this chapter) can supply your burger toppings. You go gaga for anything multipurpose, Virgo, but you'll be especially jazzed about how outstanding these burgers taste!

SERVES 4

- 1 (15-ounce) can dark red kidney beans, drained
- 1 large Yukon Gold potato, peeled, cooked, and cooled
- 1/3 cup cornmeal
- 1/3 cup fresh or defrosted frozen peas
- 2 tablespoons minced onion
- 1/4 teaspoon ground chipotle
- 1/4 teaspoon paprika
- 1/4 teaspoon ground black pepper
- 1/4 teaspoon sea salt
- 2 tablespoons apple cider vinegar
- 2 tablespoons canola oil

1. In a medium bowl, mash the beans and potato together using a potato masher. Add the remaining ingredients, except the oil. Mix and form into four patties.
2. Heat oil in a medium skillet over medium-high heat. Cook the burgers, flipping once, until cooked through and browned on both sides, about 5 minutes per side. Serve.

ANGEL HAIR WITH BROCCOLI RABE AND PECORINO CHEESE

Thoughtful Virgo, you've come to our rescue multiple times, and by now, some of us are convinced that you're an angel in disguise. Your factual mind refuses the rumors. However, you will always agree to angel hair pasta! These delicate noodles are divinely elevated with garlic, butter, and cheese, while olives give this dish the briny element that you love.

SERVES 6

---

1 cup fresh shelled fava beans
1 tablespoon olive oil
2 cloves garlic, finely chopped
⅛ teaspoon red pepper flakes
¼ cup black olives, such as
   kalamata, pitted
1 bunch broccoli rabe, cut into
   bite-sized pieces, blanched

1 pound angel hair pasta
1 tablespoon butter
¼ cup grated Parmesan cheese
1 (¼–pound) block pecorino cheese
Lemon wedges, for garnish

---

1. Bring a large pot of salted water to a rolling boil. Drop fava beans in for 2 minutes, then skim them out with a slotted spoon and shock them by plunging them into ice-cold water. Peel off the outer leathery skin. Set them aside. Keep the water at a rolling boil.

2. In a large skillet over medium heat, heat oil. Add garlic, pepper flakes, and olives and cook, stirring, until garlic begins to brown, about 1 minute. Add broccoli rabe and cook until heated through, about 2 minutes. Turn off heat.

3. Put pasta into the boiling water, stir well to separate, and cook until tender, about 5 minutes (it cooks very quickly), then drain and add to the skillet, allowing some of the water from the pasta to drip into the skillet.

4. Toss with butter and Parmesan. Divide onto serving plates. Using a swivel vegetable peeler, shave pecorino cheese liberally over pasta. Serve with lemon wedges.

STILTON-STUFFED ENDIVE

Intellectual Virgos will be intrigued by this inventive and outstandingly tasty snack. Stilton cheese is a mild and semisoft blue cheese, which serves as the base filling for this tasty snack. Roasted almonds offer the perfect salty crunch, while tart cherries add the quintessential dose of sweetness Virgos crave when snack time calls. There are different types of endive out there, but you want the oval-shaped endives, whose leaves can serve as leafy canoes for the filling. Adaptable Virgos will adore this rare and delicious combo that's paradoxically filling and light at the same time.

SERVES 10

4 medium endives
½ cup roasted almonds
½ cup dried tart cherries
1½ cups crumbled Stilton cheese

½ tablespoon minced fresh rosemary
¼ teaspoon sea salt
¼ teaspoon ground black pepper

1. Cut the ends off endives. Separate out the leaves and arrange them on a platter.
2. In a medium bowl, gently mix together almonds, cherries, cheese, rosemary, salt, and pepper.
3. Evenly distribute the mixture among the leaves, placing it on the wider end. Serve immediately.

ROASTED YUKON GOLD POTATOES

Meat and potatoes—sometimes that's all you need, Virgo. You appreciate simplicity where you can get it, so here's a solid potato standby for you to enjoy with any main dish, like the Honey-Glazed Filet Mignon (see recipe in this chapter). This dish proves that simple can also be exceptional. Baking potatoes in foil produces expertly creamy potatoes, and minimizes cleanup, but if you prefer a crispier potato, spread potatoes apart on a baking rack. You like options, Virgo. You might be picky, but you know a good thing when you see it.

SERVES 4

1 medium onion, peeled and roughly chopped
2 tablespoons olive oil
¼ cup chopped parsley
4 cloves garlic, minced

1½ pounds Yukon Gold potatoes, sliced ½" thick
1 teaspoon salt
⅛ teaspoon ground black pepper

1. Preheat oven to 425°F.
2. Put onion, olive oil, parsley, and garlic in blender or food processor and purée until smooth.
3. Place potatoes in a large bowl and toss with the onion mixture and salt. Wrap in a sheet of aluminum foil and crimp it to seal. Potatoes should be no more than two layers deep.
4. Bake on a sheet pan on center rack 45 minutes until potatoes are tender when poked with a fork. Season with pepper and serve.

◦ ◦ ◦ ◦ **COMFORT FOOD, STRAIGHT UP!** ◦ ◦ ◦ ◦

Compassionate and intelligent, Virgos are innate problem solvers who are genuinely concerned with helping people iron out their dilemmas. At the end of a long day taking care of others, Virgos will often crave some good old comfort food like roasted potatoes.

NUTTY CHICKEN FINGERS

You love cornflakes and you love chicken fingers, Virgo, but you also love creative innovation. Here's a delicious recipe that cleverly upscales these semi-youthful favorites. Cornflakes combine with chopped pecans to add a nutty, buttery, and crispy breading that meticulous Virgo will adore. The final result? Very sophisticated and seriously tasty chicken fingers. Dexterous Virgos are keen on finger food—especially a new and improved version of a childhood favorite. Dip in your preferred honey mustard and enjoy as an appetizer or as a snack.

SERVES 8

¾ cup crushed cornflake crumbs

¼ cup finely chopped pecans

2 tablespoons chopped fresh flat-leaf parsley

¼ teaspoon garlic salt

¼ teaspoon ground black pepper

4 (4-ounce) boneless, skinless chicken breasts, cut into strips about 3" long and ½" wide

3 tablespoons 1% milk

1. Preheat oven to 400°F.
2. In a shallow dish, combine cornflake crumbs, pecans, parsley, garlic salt, and pepper and mix well.
3. Dip chicken in milk, then roll in the crumb mixture to coat. Place in a 15" × 10" jelly roll pan.
4. Bake until chicken is tender, about 5–7 minutes. Serve immediately.

CALIFORNIA GARDEN SALAD WITH AVOCADO AND SPROUTS

Here's a stellar salad sure to meet Virgo's high standards. You know that details matter, so you'll truly appreciate Bibb lettuce—a salad green so luscious that it's almost buttery. Combined with creamy avocado, high-vibe sprouts, and juicy tomatoes, this fresh salad is likely to leave all earthy Virgos sincerely star struck. As if things couldn't be more perfect for you, Virgo, this recipe comes with its own simple salad dressing recipe. It doesn't get fresher than this, Virgo, so pair this salad up with the Pesto Chicken Breasts or the Homemade Bean and Vegetable Burgers (see recipes in this chapter), and you're in for a real culinary treat!

SERVES 4

1 tablespoon fresh-squeezed lemon juice
3 tablespoons extra-virgin olive oil
1 tablespoon finely chopped peeled shallot
½ teaspoon salt
¼ teaspoon ground black pepper
2 medium heads Boston or Bibb lettuce
½ pound cherry tomatoes, sliced in half
1 medium ripe avocado, peeled, pitted, and cut into 8 wedges
1 cup alfalfa sprouts

1. In a small bowl, combine lemon juice, olive oil, shallot, salt, and pepper, mixing well.
2. Arrange lettuce leaves, stem-end in, onto four plates, making a flower petal pattern. Inner leaves will be too small, so reserve them for another use.
3. Toss tomatoes in 1 tablespoon dressing; divided evenly among each salad. Toss avocado wedges with 1 tablespoon dressing. Place two wedges on each salad. Divide sprouts into four bunches and place a bunch in the center of each salad.
4. Drizzle salads with remaining dressing or serve on the side.

MISO SOUP

You're a planner, and routines are your thing. So be sure to put these specialty ingredients on your grocery list before you go shopping on Saturday morning, methodical Virgo! Miso soup is something you've eaten dozens of times, but if you've never stewed it yourself, you're in for a serious treat! Virgos love miso soup for its simplicity. It's down-to-earth, tasty, and just the thing to warm you up on a chilly day. Thoughtful Virgos will especially look forward to pairing this Miso Soup with either Tofu Summer Rolls or even the Pesto Chicken Breasts (see recipes in this chapter). Classic and simple, this is one soup every Virgo will adore.

SERVES 4

5 cups vegetable or mushroom stock
1 piece kombu, about 5" square
1 teaspoon soy sauce
3 tablespoons light (yellow) miso
2 medium scallions, chopped and
   ends trimmed

2 ounces firm tofu, diced into small
   cubes
4 teaspoons wakame seaweed (instant)
Sliced green onions, for garnish

1. In a large stockpot, bring stock and kombu to a boil. Cover; remove from heat and let stand 5 minutes. Strain; stir in soy sauce.
2. In a small bowl, mix about ¼ cup of the warm stock into miso with a wire whisk until miso is dissolved. Pour this mixture back into stockpot.
3. Place scallions, tofu, and wakame into four bowls. Gently ladle the soup into the bowls. Garnish with green onions.

∘ ∘ ∘ ∘ **KNOW YOUR GREENS** ∘ ∘ ∘ ∘

You love learning new things, Virgo, but you especially love learning hands-on. Kombu is a kelp that breaks apart easily in your Miso Soup, while wakame is a nutritious marine vegetable. Each of these green ingredients can be found in Asian specialty grocery stores or in health-food stores.

HONEY-GLAZED FILET MIGNON

Filet mignon is a no-brainer for Virgo intellectuals. This entrée is very straightforward: classy, high-quality, and supremely satisfying—especially when meticulous Virgo is manning the skillet. You can be efficient with routine tasks, Virgo, but when it comes to very important affairs (like steak), you take all the time and care you need to ensure perfection. And since it's all about the details for you, Virgo, pair your tender, juicy steak with Roasted Yukon Gold Potatoes (see recipe in this chapter), and perhaps a glass of red wine to celebrate a day well spent.

SERVES 6

6 (4-ounce) filet mignon steaks
½ teaspoon salt
⅛ teaspoon ground black pepper
1 tablespoon olive oil

3 cloves garlic, minced
2 medium shallots, peeled and minced
3 tablespoons honey
¼ cup dry red wine

1. Season steaks with salt and pepper. Heat a large nonstick skillet over medium heat and add olive oil.
2. Add steaks to pan; cook 4 minutes until easy to turn. Carefully turn steaks and cook 3–5 minutes more until desired doneness. Remove from pan and cover with foil to keep warm.
3. Turn heat to medium-high and add garlic and shallots to skillet. Cook and stir to loosen pan drippings. Add honey and wine and bring to a boil. Boil for a few minutes to reduce sauce.
4. Return steaks to pan and cook 1 minute to heat through, spooning sauce over steaks. Serve immediately.

PESTO CHICKEN BREASTS

Logical Virgos will love this straightforwardly delicious dinner. Pesto is bright and flavorful, while the chicken is baked to perfection. And that's all you ever want, practical Virgo. Simple, satisfying, and nutritious. Basil is a wonderful herb for focused Virgos to enjoy because it assists with concentration and mental clarity. Made with pine nuts and Parmesan cheese, this pesto is astronomically delicious! And since you appreciate variety, mutable Virgo, there are plenty of ways to delight in this sumptuous dish. Enjoy this chicken as is, on a sandwich, in a salad, or combined with a bed of pasta and leftover pesto.

SERVES 4

3 cups basil, loosely packed
¼ cup olive oil
¼ cup finely grated Parmesan cheese
¼ cup pine nuts

1 teaspoon kosher salt
1 teaspoon ground black pepper
4 (4-ounce) boneless, skinless chicken breasts

1. Preheat oven to 350°F.
2. Place basil, olive oil, Parmesan, pine nuts, salt, and pepper in a food processor. Pulse until a thick paste forms.
3. Line a baking sheet with foil. Rub both sides of each chicken breast with the pesto and place on baking sheet. Bake until chicken is fully cooked, about 20 minutes. Serve.

○ ○ ○ ○ PRACTICAL KITCHEN WHIZ ○ ○ ○ ○

Virgos may be practical earth signs, but they love geeking out with culinary gadgets and tools! So if you can't get enough of that pesto, Virgo, use a vacuum sealer to seal your marinated chicken for a couple of hours. This technique is said to penetrate the flavors into the meat.

TOFU SUMMER ROLLS

Here's a delicious bite that looks as impressive as it tastes! Dexterous Virgos will delight in serving their guests these superbly flavorful Tofu Summer Rolls. You love any excuse to get crafty, thoughtful Virgo, and hosting parties is where this talent shines most. The rice paper wraps might intimidate some of your other zodiac friends, Virgo, but you're gentle and meticulous enough to get the job done effortlessly. Boldly seasoned with garlic, ginger, soy sauce, and fresh basil, this is one little wrap that's sure to impress. Watch everyone's amazement when they wonder what you did to make this bite so astronomically delicious.

SERVES 6

- 1 pound extra-firm tofu, cut into 1/4" × 3" slices
- 3 tablespoons soy sauce
- 2 teaspoons rice vinegar
- 2 teaspoons ginger juice
- 2 cloves garlic, grated
- 1/2 pound rice stick noodles
- 6 rice paper wrappers
- 1/2 cup chopped steamed rainbow chard
- 3/4 cup loosely packed Thai basil

1. Place tofu in a resealable plastic bag. Add soy sauce, rice vinegar, ginger juice, and garlic. Refrigerate overnight.
2. The next day, prepare rice stick noodles and rice paper wrappers according to the package instructions.
3. Once prepared, add 1/4 cup rice noodles in the middle of each wrapper.
4. Equally divide the chard, tofu, and basil among the wrappers.
5. Fold the wrapper from both sides in toward the middle, then tightly roll the end away from you until the spring roll is closed. Serve immediately.

∘ ∘ ∘ ∘ STELLAR TOFU TECHNIQUE ∘ ∘ ∘ ∘

In a pinch, you can marinate your tofu 1 hour prior to assembly. If you really want to excel your tofu game, consider pressing it prior to wrapping. Arrange tofu in paper towels, lay a cutting board on top, followed by a filled tea kettle, and let it sit for an hour.

FISH TACOS

Virgo, you think of everything, which is why people love coming over to your house. This time, you're setting up a fabulous taco bar for your guests. Citrusy-garlicky tilapia is quick to sauté, which means that you won't have to step away from mingling for too long. Set out your taco toppings in individual bowls, allowing your guests to assemble their tacos to their liking. Multiply your recipe as necessary, and since you're so creative, Virgo, feel free to include additional toppings. The stars predict that these fresh Fish Tacos will be a surefire success at your next party, Virgo!

SERVES 6

6 (4-ounce) tilapia fillets
3 tablespoons apple cider vinegar
3 tablespoons lime juice
2 medium jalapeños, seeded and
   minced
½ teaspoon ground cumin
1 teaspoon minced garlic
½ teaspoon ground black pepper
¼ teaspoon sea salt

6 taco-sized corn tortillas, warmed
1 medium green onion, diced
¼ cup sour cream
½ pint cherry tomatoes, halved
¾ cup shredded red cabbage
1 medium avocado, peeled, pitted, and
   sliced
2 tablespoons red hot sauce

1. Place fish in a marinating container or resealable plastic bag. Add the vinegar, lime juice, jalapeños, cumin, garlic, pepper, and salt. Refrigerate 30 minutes.
2. Add the contents of the container to a medium nonstick skillet over medium heat. Sauté until fish is fully cooked, about 5–15 minutes depending on thickness.
3. Divide fish among tortillas. Top each with green onion, sour cream, tomatoes, cabbage, and avocado. Drizzle with hot sauce. Serve immediately.

BLUEBERRY RICOTTA TART

Of all the many ways to say "I love you," one of your favorite ways, dear Virgo, is with dessert. This Blueberry Ricotta Tart is sure to get the message across. Ricotta is a fluffy cheese, and with the addition of sweet honey, vanilla, and bright lemon zest, you've got the ideal pastry filling. Fresh blueberries pair perfectly with the lemony sweet cream, while the butter crumble adds a delectable dose of salted buttery texture. You appreciate these thoughtful details, Virgo, and so will your loved ones when they're lucky enough to have a slice of this tart!

SERVES 8

½ cup all-purpose flour

½ cup plus 2 tablespoons granulated sugar, divided

½ teaspoon salt, divided

⅓ cup unsalted butter, cubed and chilled

1 cup ricotta cheese

2 teaspoons lemon zest

1 teaspoon vanilla extract

2 tablespoons honey

1 large egg yolk

1 (12") round pastry crust, chilled

1 cup fresh blueberries

1. In a medium bowl, blend flour, ½ cup sugar, and ¼ teaspoon salt. Using your fingers, rub chilled butter into the mixture until the mixture resembles coarse sand. Chill this crumble 30 minutes.

2. In a large bowl, whisk together ricotta, lemon zest, vanilla, honey, 2 tablespoons sugar, egg yolk, and remaining ¼ teaspoon salt. Cover and chill 30 minutes.

3. Preheat oven to 350°F and line a baking sheet with parchment paper.

4. Place chilled pastry crust on prepared baking sheet. Spread the ricotta mixture onto the crust, leaving a ½" border.

5. Arrange blueberries over the ricotta mixture, then fold the crust just over the edge of the filling. Top with the prepared crumble.

6. Bake 45–55 minutes or until the fruit is bubbling and both the crumble and pastry are golden brown.

7. Cool to room temperature before serving.

GRAPEFRUIT COSMOPOLITAN

Virgo's favorite spirit is vodka—mainly for its versatility and its ability to mingle with a myriad of flavors. Virgos like their drinks sophisticated, yet simple, which is why these earthy logicians can always count on the cosmopolitan. Classic and sweet, this cosmo is dependable, yet open to interpretation. Virgos will enjoy this citrusy version, which maintains its usual cranberry flavor, but also showcases grapefruit flavor. This refreshing but substantial vodka drink is masterfully balanced and guaranteed to satisfy perfectionistic Virgos everywhere.

SERVES 1

1½ ounces grapefruit vodka
½ ounce Cointreau
¼ ounce lime juice or juice from a freshly squeezed lime

1 ounce cranberry juice
Lemon twist, orange twist, or lime wedge, for garnish

1. Pour all the liquid ingredients into a shaker tin of ice. Shake and strain into a cocktail glass.
2. Garnish with lemon twist, orange twist, or lime wedge.

BLONDIES

Brown sugar and butter combine in this recipe to form the butterscotch dream team that all industrious Virgos adore. While blondies are traditionally made with chocolate chips, innovative Virgos might like to experiment with butterscotch chips, toffee, M&M's, or even organic carob chips. The possibilities for sweetness are truly endless here, Virgo, which is only one reason why you'll love this recipe. Enjoy this anytime sweet treat to tide you over while you work or at the end of a big meal, or serve it in bite-sized pieces at a party.

YIELDS 36 BLONDIES

1½ cups all-purpose flour
½ teaspoon baking powder
½ teaspoon salt
6 ounces (1½ sticks) unsalted butter, at
    room temperature

1¾ cups packed brown sugar
2 teaspoons vanilla extract
3 large eggs
6 ounces (about 1 cup) semisweet
    chocolate chunks or morsels

1. Preheat oven to 350°F. Butter a 9" baking pan.
2. In a medium bowl using a stiff wire whisk, whisk together flour, baking powder, and salt.
3. In another medium bowl, combine butter, brown sugar, and vanilla and mix together using an electric mixer or by hand until light and fluffy, about 2 minutes.
4. Gradually beat in eggs to the butter mixture, working each one in completely before adding the next. Scrape down mixing bowl.
5. Add the flour mixture and beat just long enough to incorporate. Mix in chocolate chunks.
6. Transfer the batter into prepared baking pan and smooth with a spatula.
7. Bake until a toothpick inserted in the center comes out clean, about 30–35 minutes. Cool at room temperature at least 1 hour. Cut into thirty-six pieces. These will keep refrigerated for 1 week or in freezer up to 6 weeks.

Libra:
The Fancy Chef

Symbolized by the scales, Libra represents balance and fairness. These Venusian air signs are refined, charming, and intelligent, but they are way too humble to admit it. Though indecisive at times, it's easy for fair-minded Libras to see both sides of an issue. Elegant Libras have mastered the art of mediation, tact, and finding solutions that please everyone. Virtuosos of the double entendre, Libras creatively compose their lyrics in life. Ruled by magnetic Venus, social Librans have an uncanny stage presence. Libras want to be well-liked, and fortunately for them, they are easily adored.

Libra desires harmony and strives to create beauty in the world. Ruled by Venus, planet of beauty and love, this comes as no surprise! Social Libras thrive in group settings, where they can mingle, make friends, and work their charm. Plus, Libra will never say no to dressing up. As hosts, sophisticated Libras are focused on creating a beautiful environment where their guests will enjoy themselves to the max. If a Libra starlet invites you to be a guest at their table, know that they've designed the meal with you in mind. Libra's idea of a perfect meal? You guessed it! A balanced one! And yes, that includes dessert. Libra has a very demanding sweet tooth!

AUTUMN OATMEAL

Libra kicks off the autumn season in the northern hemisphere—reminiscent of leaves changing colors, back-to-school clothes, and mulled apple cider. Fortunately for you, lovely Libra, some of those warming autumn spices can be enjoyed year-round with Autumn Oatmeal. The stars are surely smiling on you this morning with this oatmeal infused with sweet cinnamon and dried currants. Oatmeal is the perfectly balanced breakfast that every Libra craves. Beauteous Libra might like to embellish the texture of this dish by adding slivered almonds or pecans for the perfect crunch. You know, for balance!

SERVES 4

---

2 cups water
1 cup rolled oats
¼ teaspoon salt
½ cup dried currants

1 teaspoon ground cinnamon
4 teaspoons honey
2 tablespoons cream
1 cup almond milk, chilled

---

1. In a medium saucepan, bring water to a boil. Add oats and salt and stir. Turn the heat to low and simmer 5 minutes.
2. Stir in currants and simmer 10 minutes, stirring occasionally.
3. Remove from heat and spoon cooked oatmeal into four bowls.
4. Sprinkle ¼ teaspoon cinnamon and drizzle 1 teaspoon honey on each bowl.
5. Combine cream with cold almond milk in a small pitcher and serve it on the side.

∘∘∘∘ CELESTIAL MATCHMAKERS ∘∘∘∘

Socially conscious Libras are adept matchmakers—and not just when it comes to romance. Libras know how to pair food and drink when it comes to any meal. Amp up the fall vibes that you love by pairing your Autumn Oatmeal with a stellar chai tea latte!

COCONUT STRAWBERRY PANCAKES

Occasionally, romantic Libras need to indulge themselves—and often with a whole crew so that no one feels left out. Chic Libras are guaranteed to feel fancy enjoying these delicious Coconut Strawberry Pancakes on a Sunday morning. Coconut gives an alluring texture to these pancakes that high-brow Libra will adore. Top with whipped cream and sliced strawberries for presentation points. This low-key luxurious breakfast is perfect for someone like you who desires that champagne experience, but this time, from the comfort of your own home.

SERVES 4

1 cup all-purpose flour
1 cup white whole-wheat flour
1½ cups 2% milk
¼ cup shredded unsweetened coconut
3 tablespoons melted unsalted butter, cooled slightly

2½ tablespoons granulated sugar
1 teaspoon vanilla extract
½ teaspoon salt
½ teaspoon baking powder
2 large eggs, beaten
⅔ cup sliced fresh strawberries

1. In a large bowl, whisk together flours, milk, coconut, butter, sugar, vanilla, salt, baking powder, and eggs until just combined. Fold in strawberries.
2. Butter or oil a hot griddle set to medium-high heat. Ladle ⅓ cup batter on the griddle for each pancake. Cook 2–3 minutes on one side or until just beginning to bubble. Flip and cook until golden. Repeat until the batter is gone. Serve immediately.

POMEGRANATE FREEZE SMOOTHIE

Blessed with a natural eye for aesthetics, artistic Libras will admire the deep currant hue of this smoothie. Beet juice, pomegranate juice, and blueberries combine to deliver a sipper that's as delicious as it is beautiful. Imbued with potent health benefits, this smoothie is packed with antioxidants, minerals, and vitamins. Beets are here to support liver and kidney functions—the very organs belonging to Libra's domain in the body.

YIELDS 1½ CUPS

¾ cup fresh beet juice
¾ cup fresh pomegranate juice
1 cup blueberries

2 tablespoons raw honey
1 cup ice

1. Combine all the ingredients in a blender and process until smooth.
2. Serve immediately.

∘∘∘∘ PERFECTLY SWEET ∘∘∘∘

Amiable Libras have an undeniable sweet tooth, but they also appreciate bitter profiles. This smoothie strikes the perfect balance of bitter and sweet, but if it's not quite sweet enough for you, Libra, go ahead and add half of a banana.

HEALTHY VEGETABLE CUBAN

Balanced Libras will adore the equilibrium of vibrant flavors in this outstanding Healthy Vegetable Cuban sandwich. Traditional Cubans include ham and roasted pork, but this vegetable version replaces them with baked vegetables and homemade hummus.

SERVES 1

½ large portobello mushroom, sliced
¼ medium zucchini, sliced lengthwise
¼ medium yellow squash, sliced lengthwise
¼ medium red bell pepper, seeded and sliced
⅛ teaspoon salt

⅛ teaspoon ground black pepper
1 (4") portion Cuban bread
1 tablespoon Roasted Red Pepper Hummus (see sidebar)
1 teaspoon yellow mustard
1 (1-ounce) slice Swiss cheese
1 slice sour pickle

1. Preheat oven to 400°F.
2. Coat a sheet pan with cooking spray and add mushroom, zucchini, squash, and bell pepper. Season with salt and pepper.
3. Bake 8 minutes, flip vegetables, then cook about 6–8 minutes or until brown.
4. Remove vegetables from pan and refrigerate at least 1 hour.
5. Slice bread in half. Spread hummus on top half and mustard on the bottom.
6. Top bottom half with vegetables, cheese, and pickle, then cover with top.
7. Coat a medium skillet with cooking spray and place over medium heat. Place the sandwich in pan and cook each side for 3 minutes. Serve.

∘ ∘ ∘ ∘ ROASTED RED PEPPER HUMMUS ∘ ∘ ∘ ∘

To make your own delicious Roasted Red Pepper Hummus just take: 1 (15-ounce) can chickpeas (drained), ⅓ cup tahini, ⅔ cup chopped roasted red peppers, 3 tablespoons lemon juice, 2 tablespoons olive oil, 2 cloves garlic, ½ teaspoon ground cumin, ⅓ teaspoon salt, and ¼ teaspoon cayenne pepper (optional). Then simply process all the ingredients together in a blender or food processor until smooth, scraping the sides down as needed. Makes about 1½ cups hummus.

TEMPEH "CHICKEN" SALAD

Cultured Libra will often indulge in foods from all over the world, but sometimes the foods they eat are literally cultured. Tempeh is a firm, high-protein nosh created with fermented soybeans and can be found in almost any grocery store. This tempeh salad boasts an ideal balance of all Libra's favorite flavor profiles: It's creamy, it's crunchy, and it has the perfect low-key supporting notes of sweet and sour. For those days when you can't decide what to eat, indecisive Libra, you need a dish that has it all. So look no further than this Tempeh "Chicken" Salad! Enjoy in a pita sandwich or serve on top of salad greens.

SERVES 4

1 (8-ounce) package tempeh, diced small
3 tablespoons vegan mayonnaise
2 teaspoons lemon juice
½ teaspoon garlic powder
1 teaspoon Dijon mustard

2 tablespoons sweet pickle relish
½ cup fresh green peas
2 medium stalks celery, diced small
1 tablespoon chopped fresh dill (optional)

1. In a small saucepan, cover tempeh with water, bring to a boil and then reduce heat and simmer 10 minutes until tempeh is soft. Drain and allow to cool completely.
2. In a medium bowl, whisk together mayonnaise, lemon juice, garlic powder, mustard, and relish.
3. Add cooked tempeh, peas, celery, and dill if using and gently toss to combine.
4. Chill at least 1 hour before serving to allow flavors to combine.

RICOTTA CROSTINI

Elegant Libras like to be fancy, but they also know that some things in life should be easy. Here's a snack that lets you indulge in the best of both worlds, harmonious Libra. Divinely soft ricotta cheese spreads evenly onto the toasted baguette slices, while peppery radish slices add a necessary crunch component to this snack. This easy and classy snack is just the thing to hold you over, social Libra, as you entertain guests or breeze about through your day.

SERVES 8

1 medium baguette, sliced
10 ounces fresh ricotta

12 medium red radishes, thinly sliced
½ cup chopped chives

1. Preheat oven to 300°F.
2. Place baguette slices in a single layer on a baking sheet. Bake 5 minutes or until lightly toasted. Remove from oven and allow to cool.
3. Spread baguette slices with fresh ricotta. Top with radish slices. Sprinkle with chives. Serve.

HALIBUT CEVICHE

Elegant Libras will surely feel chic when they serve up this popular coastal delicacy. Ceviche is an iconic dish featuring fresh fish that's cured in citrus juices and accentuated with hot peppers. Ceviche's origin is claimed by Peru, though this citrusy dish is enjoyed in coastal regions all over the world. Amiable Libras don't shy away from overtly bold citrus sour flavors. The stars predict overwhelming taste bud satisfaction for you, classy Libra, so grab one of your salad forks and dig in!

SERVES 4

1½–2 pounds fresh halibut
½ cup lime juice
1 small red onion, peeled and cut into
   ¼" pieces
2 serrano chilies, seeded and cut into
   ¼" pieces

1 large red tomato, cored and cut into
   ¼" pieces, juice reserved
½ cup chopped fresh cilantro leaves
½ cup orange juice
1 teaspoon salt

1. Cut halibut into ½" cubes. Combine fish and lime juice in a small glass or ceramic container. Cover and refrigerate 1 hour.
2. Drain off and discard lime juice and put fish in a medium-sized mixing bowl. Add onion, chilies, tomato with juice, cilantro, orange juice, and salt; stir well.
3. Refrigerate in a glass or ceramic container 4–12 hours before serving.

∘ ∘ ∘ ∘ **SOPHISTICATED CEVICHE** ∘ ∘ ∘ ∘

Libra is not one to be intimidated by something bold or new, but what if your guests scoff at "raw" fish? Simply explain that the fish is effectively and lightly "cooked" in citrus juice. As you are a Libra with fine polished tastes, you have already chosen the freshest halibut you can find, so reassure your guests it is safe and delicious to eat.

PUERTO RICAN GANDULES
(Pigeon Peas)

Libra, you know a good match when you see it, which is why you'll take these delicious gandules and mix them with their perfect partner, rice. Traditionally, gandules are served with pork and long-grain white rice (which later takes on a signature golden tone from the sofrito). Once you've finished the steps in this recipe, begin boiling 2 cups of rice and cook to your preference. Then, using your eye for perfect proportions, cordial Libra, mix the cooked gandules and rice together and serve!

SERVES 6

1½ cups pigeon peas, soaked overnight, rinsed, and drained
1 tablespoon olive oil
1 small Spanish onion, peeled and chopped
⅓ medium green bell pepper, seeded and chopped
2 cloves garlic, minced

2 bay leaves
1½ teaspoons salt
¼ teaspoon ground black pepper
¼ cup chopped fresh thyme or 1 tablespoon dried
1 medium tomato, cored, seeded, and chopped

1. Simmer pigeon peas in 4 cups water for 1 hour until tender.
2. Meanwhile, heat olive oil in a 10" skillet over medium-high heat, then add onion, bell pepper, garlic, bay leaves, salt, black pepper, and thyme and sauté until onion is translucent (about 5 minutes). Add tomato and cook 2 minutes more.
3. Add peas to the vegetables and cook 45 minutes more until peas are very soft, then serve (discard bay leaves first, though).

∘ ∘ ∘ ∘ BETTER TOGETHER ∘ ∘ ∘ ∘

According to Libra, two minds are always better than one. These socialites thrive in group settings and are constantly initiating the weekend plans. Libran matchmakers are also highly qualified in pairing dishes—so you can look forward to serving these gandules with the Halibut Ceviche or the Chipotle Lime Duck with Chipotle Cherry Sauce (see recipes in this chapter) for a complete meal.

LAMB WITH GARLIC, LEMON, AND ROSEMARY

Posh Libras adore an excuse to get fancy, but there better be a good reason for it. Tonight, that reason is roasted lamb. Poise yourself, Libra. Dishes this elegant call for your signature finesse. You'll elevate this dish by roasting the lamb low and slow. You might even like to apply your rub several hours in advance, allowing for deeper integration of your flavors. Lamb is traditionally served with a mint sauce or a mint jelly, so charming Librans might like to pair this dish with their Spinach Salad with Apples and Mint (see recipe in this chapter). Leave it to you to go all out on dinner, sophisticated Libra!

SERVES 4

4 cloves garlic, crushed
1½ tablespoons chopped fresh
   rosemary, divided
1 tablespoon olive oil
½ teaspoon salt

1 teaspoon ground black pepper
1 (3-pound) leg of lamb
1 large lemon, cut into ¼" slices
½ cup red wine

1. In a small bowl, mix together garlic, 1 tablespoon rosemary, olive oil, salt, and pepper. Rub this mixture onto lamb.
2. Spray a 4- to 5-quart slow cooker with olive oil cooking spray. Place a few lemon slices in the bottom of slow cooker. Place spice-rubbed lamb on top of lemon slices.
3. Add remaining lemon slices on top of lamb. Pour wine around lamb.
4. Cook on low 8–10 hours or on high 4–6 hours. Serve garnished with lemon slices and remaining rosemary.

SMOKY, SPICY DEVILED EGGS

Objective Librans are known to play devil's advocate, which is why you're serving deviled eggs! Fair-minded Libran starlets are adept at entertaining multiple POVs (yes, even the devil's), so it's no coincidence that you're serving the ultimate hors d'oeuvre that absolutely everyone can agree upon. You understand that it's just not a party without these quintessential, creamy, handheld egg halves, socialite Libra. This recipe replaces mayonnaise with high-protein Greek yogurt, lending even more fluffiness to your filling, while chipotle adds a lightly smoky sweetness that balanced Libra is sure to adore. This one's a crowd-pleaser, Libra, and your party guests will surely agree!

SERVES 24
---

12 large hard-boiled eggs, peeled
¼ cup plain Greek yogurt
1 tablespoon Dijon mustard
½ teaspoon smoked paprika, plus extra
    for garnish

¼ teaspoon ground chipotle
⅛ teaspoon ground white pepper
⅛ teaspoon sea salt

---

1. Halve eggs lengthwise. Place the yolks in a small bowl. Set the whites aside. Mash the yolks with a potato masher until fluffy.
2. In a small bowl, whisk together yogurt, mustard, and spices. Scrape the mixture into the bowl of yolks. Use a fork to beat the mixture into the yolks until smooth.
3. Pipe or spoon the mixture into the whites. Sprinkle with additional paprika for garnish.

BAKED SMOKED HAM

When it comes to parties, classy Librans dress to impress—and their dishes are just as elegant. That's why Libra shows up with a holiday ham, even if it's just a casual family brunch. Any social gathering is a holiday for you, friendly Libra. Artistic Libra will enjoy bedazzling the diamond markings on the ham with bitter herbal cloves—because as any Libra knows, a beautiful dish is a tastier dish. Salty ham pairs divinely with this sweet glaze. We're using apple in this recipe, but feel free to try an orange or pineapple glaze.

SERVES 10

1 (5-pound) smoked ham
¼–½ cup cloves
½ cup apple juice

½ cup honey
½ cup Dijon mustard

1. Preheat oven to 350°F.
2. Score the outside of the ham from one end to the other, making lines about 1" apart. Repeat in the opposite direction, making a diamond pattern on the ham.
3. Place ham in a large baking dish. Insert a clove at every corner where the scored lines intersect. (The round part of the cloves should be sticking out of the ham.)
4. In a medium bowl, mix together juice, honey, and mustard. Spoon the glaze over ham.
5. Cover and bake 1½ hours. Uncover and bake 30 more minutes. Remove cloves before serving.

CHOCOLATE MOUSSE

Here's a smooth, sensual dessert that will make any chic Libran melt. Every Venusian adores a rich Chocolate Mousse, so this one's for you, elegant Libra! Romantic Librans can feel fancy whipping up this delectable French dessert, but obviously the most enjoyable part comes afterward. Yum! This dessert needs to chill in the refrigerator for a minimum of 6 hours, allowing you to tend to other more important Libra matters while you wait—like commenting on all your acquaintances' social media posts. This silky dessert calls for your signature sultry finesse, Libra, so get ready to bring it!

SERVES 8

- 1½ tablespoons Kirschwasser or cherry brandy
- 1½ tablespoons dark rum (such as Myers's)
- 1 tablespoon plus a few drops vanilla extract, divided
- 6 ounces dark (bittersweet) chocolate
- 1½ cups heavy cream
- 2½ tablespoons confectioners' sugar
- 6 large egg whites, whipped to medium-soft peaks, refrigerated
- 8 small mint leaves.

1. Chill eight 8-ounce dessert dishes.
2. Combine cherry brandy, dark rum, 1 tablespoon vanilla, and chocolate in a double boiler (or a steel mixing bowl set over a pot of simmering water). Warm, stirring occasionally, until melted and smooth.
3. In a medium bowl, whip together cream, confectioners' sugar, and a few drops vanilla until the mixture forms soft peaks when the whisk is lifted from it.
4. Gently fold ⅓ of the whipped cream into the chocolate mixture. Fold the chocolate mixture back into the rest of the whipped cream, mixing only as much as is necessary to incorporate it most of the way (a few streaks of chocolate are okay).
5. Fold whipped egg whites very gently into the chocolate cream mixture just barely enough to incorporate. Fill the mousse into a pastry bag with a star tip (or a plastic bag with a corner cut out) and pipe it into the chilled dishes.
6. Cover the dishes individually with plastic wrap and chill at least 6 hours until set. Garnish each dish with a mint leaf.

CRANBERRY WALNUT CAKE

Every beauteous Libra looks forward to dessert. With sweet-toothed Venus as your planetary ruler, you aim for desserts that are as divine to look at as they are to eat. Bittersweet cranberries dot this cake batter with vibrant bursts of juicy red fruit, while walnuts offer a subtle texture to this cake that balanced Libra will love. Not sweet enough, you say? Ice with a white chocolate drizzle. This cake is easy to make and gorgeous enough to serve at holiday parties, but it's totally enjoyable any day of the week—because you never know when that sweet tooth is going to call, Libra.

SERVES 14

½ cup unsalted butter, at room temperature
1½ cups light brown sugar
½ cup milk, at room temperature
3 large eggs, at room temperature
8 ounces sour cream, at room temperature
1 teaspoon vanilla bean paste

2 cups all-purpose flour
1 cup white whole-wheat flour
1 teaspoon baking soda
1 teaspoon baking powder
¼ teaspoon salt
½ cup halved walnuts
12 ounces cranberries

1. Preheat oven to 350°F. Grease a Bundt pan.
2. In a large bowl, cream together butter and brown sugar. Once combined, add milk, eggs, sour cream, and vanilla paste. Beat until smooth.
3. In a medium bowl, whisk together flours, baking soda, baking powder, and salt. Slowly stream the mixture into the wet ingredients until well incorporated. Fold in walnuts and cranberries.
4. Pour the batter into prepared pan. Bake 55 minutes or until a thin knife inserted into the middle of the cake comes out clean.
5. Cool 5 minutes in the pan, then remove and cool completely on a wire rack.

FRENCH 75

Charismatic Libras are always enticed by a gorgeous cocktail. For these Venusians, the prettier something looks, the more delicious it will taste. The elegant golden hue of the French 75 certainly delivers! Librans will be charmed by the citrus notes of this sophisticated concoction. Topped with chilled champagne, this is one fizzy sip that will make Libra feel downright classy. Libra has their choice of dry or sweet champagne depending on what else is on the menu. Pair with the Coconut Strawberry Pancakes for a stellar brunch, or the Ricotta Crostini for the perfect happy hour (see recipes in this chapter)!

SERVES 1

1 ounce gin
1 ounce lemon juice
½ ounce simple syrup

Chilled champagne to fill
1 lemon twist

1. Build gin, lemon juice, and simple syrup into a champagne flute and top with chilled champagne.
2. Garnish with lemon twist.

Scorpio:
The Enigmatic Chef

The most veiled and complex sign of the zodiac is, without a doubt, you, mysterious Scorpio! These watery scorpions have an enigmatic intrigue that is as fascinating as it is fierce. And to be honest, Scorpio loves that they slightly intimidate people. These private water signs are careful not to reveal too much of themselves until trust is established. "All or nothing" applies to everything in their lives, including relationships, reserving their loyal gaze only for the worthiest of endeavors. Ruled by desirous Mars, Scorpios are driven by their passions.

Enchanting Scorpios always bring their intensity to the kitchen. "All-out or take-out," as they say. If Scorpio has a craving for a dish, they will stop at nothing to achieve it. The electric mixer breaks mid-batter? Resourceful Scorpio miraculously attaches the whisk to a power drill. Celestial scorpions also love a dish with a sting! So you can look forward to Garlic-Studded Pork Roast or Jamaican Red Bean Stew. Spicy foods benefit this fierce fixed water sign, so it's a good thing that these starry arachnids are poised to stand the heat! As hosts, devoted Scorpios revel in devising intimate candlelit dinners with their closest friends or wooing their love interests with their stealth culinary prowess. So if you're invited to dine with Scorpio, know that you're in for an unforgettable treat!

CHILAQUILES

Rise and shine, stellar Scorpio! Pronounced "chee-la-KEY-lehs," this popular Mexican breakfast scramble boasts a captivating concoction of creaminess and smoky spices, sure to enthrall magnetic Scorpios everywhere. Tortilla chips for breakfast? Yes, dear scorpion. There's no such thing as waste in your house. Co-ruled by the regenerative powers of Pluto, Scorpios are masters of upcycling, repurposing, and composting. So for those times when you still have half a bag of tortilla chips, you know what to do: Jump-start your day with Chilaquiles—the perfect high-protein breakfast to put the fire in your belly.

SERVES 2

---

4 cups tortilla chips
2 cups vegetable stock, as needed
1 cup spicy tomato sauce
2 tablespoons butter

4 large eggs
2 tablespoons sour cream
2 tablespoons chopped fresh cilantro,
   for garnish

---

1. In a large skillet over high heat, place chips. Add 1 cup vegetable stock and tomato sauce. Bring to a boil, then lower to a simmer, adding more stock as needed to keep the mixture soupy. Cook until the tortillas are softened but not mushy, about 5–7 minutes.
2. In a separate large skillet over medium heat, melt butter. Cook eggs over easy in melted butter.
3. Serve the chilaquiles on two plates, topped with fried eggs, a dollop of sour cream, and a sprinkling of cilantro.

∘ ∘ ∘ ∘ **GO ALL OUT** ∘ ∘ ∘ ∘

Enigmatic scorpions have a penchant for details and tend to go all-in on a dish. Once you've got the basics down, feel free to add refried beans, sliced avocado, or top with queso fresco. The possibilities are endless here. Let your stomach lead, Scorpio, and don't hold back on your creative whims! Any way you slice it, you can't go wrong with this delectable Mexican breakfast!

BLUEBERRY CORNMEAL PANCAKES

As a Scorpio, you love corn bread muffins, so you'll absolutely adore these tasty griddle cakes. Cornmeal's texture may be denser than flour, but it's also more nutritious and higher in fiber. Antioxidant-rich blueberries add a pop of color and a lovable low-key sweetness that sensual Scorpio will adore. This is one breakfast you can trust to adequately fuel you in the morning, Scorpio. Drizzle with maple syrup and a touch of butter, and prepare to be unstoppable!

SERVES 4

1 cup all-purpose flour
1/2 cup yellow cornmeal
3 tablespoons granulated sugar
1 1/2 teaspoons baking powder
1/2 teaspoon baking soda

1/2 teaspoon salt
2 large eggs
3 tablespoons butter, melted
1 1/2 cups buttermilk
1 cup blueberries

1. In a large bowl, whisk together flour, cornmeal, sugar, baking powder, baking soda, and salt.
2. In a medium bowl, whisk together eggs, melted butter, and buttermilk.
3. Stir the egg mixture into the flour mixture until combined. There will be lumps; be careful not to overmix.
4. Pour about 1/3 cup batter for each pancake onto a hot oiled griddle or pan. Scatter several blueberries over the batter. Flip pancakes when bubbles have formed and started to pop through the batter on top, about 3–5 minutes.
5. Cook on second side about 1–2 minutes. Serve hot.

BLACK RASPBERRY AND VANILLA SMOOTHIE

Spellbinding scorpions are never afraid of the dark, which is why you're craving a smoothie made with the darkest of fruits: blackberries. Also featuring raspberries and silky vanilla yogurt, this impeccably delicious smoothie is sure to enchant Scorpios everywhere with its hypnotic purple hue and irresistible creaminess. But resilient scorpions take heed: Delicate berries are so divinely juicy that if you don't eat them right away, they are prone to mold. Don't take such risks, determined Scorpio. Instead, rinse your berries and keep them in the freezer until your blackberry craving calls.

YIELDS 1½ CUPS

2 cups blackberries
½ cup raspberries

1 cup low-fat vanilla yogurt
2 tablespoons raw honey

1. Combine all the ingredients in a blender and purée until smooth.
2. Serve immediately.

° ° ° ° HIDDEN POWERS ° ° ° °

Scorpios have their ways of knowing. Chalk it up to their keen perception or psychic powers, but either way you slice it, these mysterious scorpions have a penchant for seeing the unseen. This detective skill comes in handy in the kitchen! Scorpios often "sense" when their food finished cooking, and they even "feel out" which onion they should buy.

MONTE CRISTO SANDWICHES

We always feel your presence when you walk into the room, magnetic Scorpio, but this time you'll be turning heads with these Monte Cristo Sandwiches. They're traditionally served with ham, turkey, and Swiss, but this recipe takes a suspenseful turn with crispy bacon, seared chicken breast, and Gouda. Sensual Scorpios will be transfixed by this slightly sinful sandwich. Did we mention there's raspberry jam involved? For someone like you who likes to go all out, these Monte Cristo Sandwiches will undoubtedly meet all your lunchtime desires.

SERVES 4

4 slices bacon
2 (4-ounce) boneless, skinless chicken
   breasts
¼ cup raspberry jam

8 slices white bread
8 thin slices Gouda cheese
4 (1-ounce) slices ham
¼ cup butter, softened

1. In a medium skillet over medium-high heat, cook bacon until crisp. Remove from pan and drain on paper towels; crumble and set aside. Pour off drippings from skillet and discard; do not wipe skillet.
2. Reduce heat to medium and add chicken to skillet. Cook, turning once, until browned and cooked, about 8 minutes. Remove chicken from pan and let stand.
3. Spread jam on one side of each slice of bread. Layer half of the bread slices with cheese and then ham. Thinly slice chicken breasts and place over ham. Cover with remaining cheese slices, sprinkle with bacon, and top the sandwiches with remaining bread slices.
4. Spread outsides of the sandwiches with softened butter. Prepare and preheat griddle, indoor dual-contact grill, or panini maker. Grill sandwiches on medium 4–6 minutes for dual-contact grill or panini maker, or 6–8 minutes, turning once, for griddle until bread is golden brown and cheese is melted. Cut in half and serve immediately.

CHICKEN SAGE BURGERS

Superstitious scorpions might regularly burn sage to clear the energy in their home, but they also adore this notorious bitter herb as a seasoning. Sage is an ideal herb pairing for chicken—just ask fellow Scorpio, and famed Michelin-starred chef, Gordon Ramsay! It takes a lot to impress you, dear Scorpio, but these mouthwatering Chicken Sage Burgers are sure to entice—whether served on a bun or over a bed of greens. Stomach satisfaction is written in the stars for you today, Scorpio!

SERVES 4

1 pound ground chicken breast
1 medium shallot, peeled and minced
½ cup fresh whole-wheat bread crumbs
1 tablespoon creamy mustard
1 tablespoon champagne vinegar
2 tablespoons minced sage
1 clove garlic, minced
4 slices fontina cheese
4 hamburger buns

1. In a medium bowl, with a gentle hand, mix together chicken, shallot, bread crumbs, mustard, vinegar, sage, and garlic. Form into four equal-sized, flattish patties.
2. Spray a medium skillet with nonstick cooking spray and place over medium-high heat. Cook the burgers, turning once, until fully cooked, about 10–15 minutes.
3. Add a slice of cheese to each, cook 30 seconds or until cheese is starting to melt. Serve on buns.

○ ○ ○ ○ WHICH SAGE IS WHICH? ○ ○ ○ ○

We don't recommend seasoning your chicken with your smudge stick. Truth be told, there are hundreds of varieties of sage growing all over the world. Common sage, or culinary sage, is what you're looking to stock in your spice cabinet. Keep your white sage next to your crystal collection instead!

APRICOT OAT CAKES

*You're tough and you're strong, Scorpio, but every once in a blue moon,
you need some sweetness in your life. On your own terms, of course. Which
is why you're whipping up Apricot Oat Cakes. Energizing, high in protein,
and out-of-this-world tasty, these sweet oat bites are just what you need
to flawlessly sail over that last hump of the workday. Enjoy these sweet
cookie cakes with an afternoon coffee or an Earl Grey latte. Not feeling the
sweetness today, enigmatic Scorpio? Feel free to swap the sugar
for chia seeds instead.*

SERVES 8

3 cups rolled oats
2 cups all-purpose flour
¼ teaspoon baking powder
1 large egg white
⅓ cup plain yogurt

½ cup granulated sugar
½ cup honey
½ teaspoon vanilla extract
½ cup chopped dried apricots

1. Preheat oven to 325°F. Line a baking sheet with parchment paper.
2. Pulse oats in a food processor ten times, then add flour and baking powder
   and pulse to mix.
3. In a large bowl, whisk egg white until frothy, then add yogurt, sugar, honey, and
   vanilla. Add the oat mixture and dried apricots to the yogurt mixture. Mix with
   a wooden spoon.
4. Roll the mixture into eight balls and flatten them into thick, cylindrical patties.
5. Bake on prepared baking sheet 15–20 minutes. Let cool and refrigerate unless
   eating right away.

ROASTED CARROTS WITH HONEY AND THYME

Alluring Scorpios are always down for a "good thyme"—and this time, your favorite savory herb is here to elevate another one of your favorites, roasted carrots! Honey gives these carrots their irresistible glaze, while dry white wine expertly softens the carrots and brings the vital acidic element that all Scorpios seek. If you don't have a zester, no worries, resourceful Scorpio; a vegetable peeler works great. This dish is the perfect accompaniment to the Garlic-Studded Pork Roast (see recipe in this chapter), as well as many other stellar dishes the stars foresee in your future.

SERVES 4

8 medium carrots, peeled
⅓ cup extra-virgin olive oil
1 teaspoon grated orange zest
1 tablespoon honey

2 tablespoons dry white wine
1 teaspoon salt
½ teaspoon ground black pepper
2 teaspoons fresh thyme leaves

1. Preheat oven to 400°F.
2. In a large bowl, combine carrots, oil, zest, honey, wine, salt, pepper, and thyme. Stir to coat. Empty the contents of the bowl evenly onto a baking tray.
3. Bake 25–30 minutes or until tender. Serve immediately or at room temperature.

CHICKEN TENDERS WITH HONEY MUSTARD DIPPING SAUCE

Spellbinding Scorpios are strong, but if there's one thing they can't resist, it's the crispy allure of fried chicken. Don't hold back on this one, Scorpio. With the perfect amount of spice, and breaded to perfection, these Chicken Tenders are a nosh that you will adore at any time of the day. Enjoy as a snack or an appetizer or on top of a stack of waffles. And for ambitious Scorpios seeking an extra potent sting? Add an extra teaspoon of cayenne pepper.

SERVES 6

2 pounds boneless, skinless chicken breasts, cut into 1"-wide strips
1 tablespoon ground black pepper
½ tablespoon kosher salt
2 teaspoons garlic powder
1 teaspoon hot paprika
1½ teaspoons ground mustard powder
½ teaspoon chili powder
1 cup all-purpose flour
2½ cups panko
3 large eggs, beaten
Canola oil, for frying
¾ cup mayonnaise
2 tablespoons honey
2 tablespoons Dijon mustard
½ tablespoon lemon juice

1. In a large bowl, toss chicken strips with pepper, salt, garlic powder, paprika, mustard powder, and chili powder. Set aside.
2. Place flour, panko, and eggs in three separate shallow bowls. Dip chicken in the flour, then the egg, and finally the panko.
3. Meanwhile, heat 2" canola oil in a deep skillet or Dutch oven over medium heat. Fry chicken until golden brown, about 3–5 minutes per side. Drain on paper towel–lined plates.
4. In a small bowl, whisk together mayonnaise, honey, mustard, and lemon juice. Serve chicken immediately with this dipping sauce.

JAMAICAN RED BEAN STEW

Celestial scorpions treasure a hearty stew. So here's an astronomically delicious stew to warm your belly and your heart! Jamaican Red Bean Stew delivers the spicy kick you crave, while its sweet potatoes and creamy coconut milk bring a delicate sweetness to this soup that jibes well with the jerk seasonings. This soup cooks low and slow, allowing the flavors to finesse on their own. While you wait for your soup to stew, you can tend to more important Scorpio matters—like counting pennies or Internet stalking your ex. So strategic of you, stealthy Scorpio.

SERVES 4

---

2 tablespoons olive oil
½ medium onion, peeled and diced
2 cloves garlic, minced
1 (15-ounce) can diced tomatoes
3 cups diced sweet potatoes
2 (15-ounce) cans red kidney beans, drained

1 cup coconut milk
3 cups vegetable broth
2 teaspoons jerk seasoning
2 teaspoons curry powder
⅛ teaspoon salt
⅛ teaspoon ground black pepper

---

1. In a medium sauté pan over medium heat, add olive oil, then sauté onion and garlic about 3 minutes.
2. Transfer the mixture to a 4-quart slow cooker, and add all the remaining ingredients. Cover and cook on low heat 6 hours.
3. Stir and serve.

◦ ◦ ◦ ◦ **HOORAY FOR LEFTOVERS!** ◦ ◦ ◦ ◦

Cosmic scorpions are also acutely aware of how valuable their time is—that's why when Scorpio has a busy week ahead, they are content doubling their recipe and eating the same meal for a few days. Fortunately for you, Scorpio, this stew is so delicious that you'll be happy to dip in on the daily!

TOFU SALAD WITH GINGER MISO DRESSING

Here's a salad that will make everyone else at the lunch table green with envy, Scorpio. Ginger is an energizing and anti-inflammatory spice that belongs under the domain of Mars, Scorpio's ruler. Ginger costars with miso paste in the making of this stellar dressing guaranteed to beguile magnetic Scorpios. If you prefer crispier tofu you might like to slice your cubes smaller, making them 1/2". Or maybe tofu isn't your thing at all? Not to fret. This marinade is as steady as they come. Go ahead and try it out with another of your favorite proteins.

SERVES 4

GINGER MISO DRESSING

1 tablespoon soy sauce
1 tablespoon miso paste
1/4 cup rice wine vinegar
1/2 tablespoon granulated sugar
1 teaspoon sesame oil
1 tablespoon toasted sesame seeds
1 tablespoon minced ginger
1 teaspoon minced garlic
1/4 teaspoon ground black pepper
1/4 cup vegetable oil

SALAD

2 tablespoons low-sodium soy sauce
1 tablespoon honey
1 teaspoon sesame oil
2 medium scallions, diced and ends trimmed
2 cloves garlic, minced
4 tablespoons vegetable oil, divided
1 (12.3-ounce) block firm tofu, dried with paper towels, cut into 1" cubes
8 cups mixed greens
1 cup sliced cucumbers
1/2 cup shredded peeled carrots
3 medium Roma tomatoes, cored, seeded, and quartered
1/2 small red onion, peeled and thinly sliced
1 teaspoon toasted sesame seeds

1. In a blender, combine all the dressing ingredients except vegetable oil. Pulse several times until the ingredients have broken down.
2. On the lowest setting, slowly stream in oil and blend until dressing is fully emulsified. Set aside.

3. In a medium bowl, whisk together soy sauce, honey, sesame oil, scallions, garlic, and 2 tablespoons vegetable oil. Add tofu cubes to the bowl and toss to coat. Refrigerate 1 hour.
4. Divide mixed greens among four bowls. Top each bowl with cucumbers, carrots, tomatoes, and onion.
5. Heat remaining vegetable oil in a wok over medium heat. Add tofu and stir-fry 2–3 minutes until cubes have become golden brown. Divide tofu cubes among the four bowls.
6. Drizzle the Ginger Miso Dressing over the salads and sprinkle with toasted sesame seeds.

∘ ∘ ∘ ∘ **MARVELOUS MISO** ∘ ∘ ∘ ∘

Your guests will be amazed by the delicious and complex flavors in this salad. The dressing revolves around the principles of balancing salty, sweet, sour, spicy, and bitter flavors. The miso paste, which is a paste made from fermented soybeans, brings a unique burst of salty and tangy to this dressing and many other Asian dishes. It is the star of this dish, just like you, Scorpio!

GINGER PEANUT NOODLES

Your love and attention are exclusive prizes, Scorpio. Not everyone is deserving of your loyalty, but here's a dish deserving of your unwavering devotion: Ginger Peanut Noodles. Spellbinding Scorpios will be particularly obsessed with this Thai-inspired peanut sauce—salty, sweet, and spicy in all the right ways, unified with brightening lime juice. Looking to add a protein? How about some marinated tofu or a side of Chicken Tenders with Honey Mustard Dipping Sauce (see recipe in this chapter)?

SERVES 6

¾ cup smooth peanut butter
1 tablespoon honey
⅓ cup low-sodium soy sauce
¼ cup rice wine vinegar
1½ tablespoons toasted sesame oil
1½ tablespoons sambal chili paste
2 tablespoons minced ginger
1 tablespoon minced garlic
1 teaspoon lime zest
½ tablespoon fresh lime juice

¼ cup water
1 pound Shanghai noodles
2 tablespoons vegetable oil
2 tablespoons minced shallots
½ teaspoon red pepper flakes
2 medium scallions, cut into 1" strips
   and ends trimmed
¼ cup crushed roasted peanuts
1 teaspoon toasted sesame seeds

1. In a blender, combine peanut butter, honey, soy sauce, vinegar, sesame oil, sambal, ginger, garlic, lime zest, and lime juice. Blend until smooth. Add water if sauce is too thick. Set aside.
2. Fill a large pot with water and bring to a boil. Add noodles and cook 1–2 minutes. Drain noodles in a colander and reserve ¼ cup of the starchy water.
3. In a wok, heat vegetable oil over medium heat and toss in shallots. Stir-fry shallots 30 seconds before adding red pepper flakes and cooked noodles. Stir-fry an additional 30 seconds.
4. Ladle in 2–3 spoonfuls of peanut sauce at a time until noodles have been thoroughly coated. Add 1–2 tablespoons of the starchy water to loosen the sauce. Toss in scallions and stir-fry an additional 30 seconds. Plate noodles and top them with peanuts and sesame seeds.

GARLIC-STUDDED PORK ROAST

Intense Scorpios are passionate people who prefer a dish that comes on strong. This Garlic-Studded Pork Roast is here to satisfy. Complete with an entire bulb of garlic (yes, the whole thing!), fierce Scorpios can take comfort that this flavorful roast holds nothing back. Scorpio's ruling planet, Mars, also governs pungent garlic. Garlic is a powerful remedial weapon that's been used to strengthen the immune system, and is also megadelicious. Maybe don't whip this one up for a hot date, though, especially if your date is a sultry vampire. Hey, we never know with you, enchanting Scorpio!

SERVES 8

1 (2-pound) pork loin
1 bulb garlic, peeled
1 cup fresh basil leaves
1 cup fresh Italian parsley
2 tablespoons olive oil

¼ cup lemon juice
2 tablespoons lemon zest
1 teaspoon sea salt
1 teaspoon ground black pepper

1. Preheat oven to 350°F.
2. Cut slits on all sides of pork and insert a garlic clove in each one.
3. Place basil, parsley, olive oil, lemon juice, zest, salt, and pepper in a food processor. Pulse until a paste forms.
4. Rub the paste over the pork. Place in a Dutch oven and roast 40 minutes or until pork is fully cooked. Let pork stand before slicing and serving.

ROASTED RED PEPPER DIP

You might prefer to keep a low profile, enigmatic Scorpio, but you really know how to captivate an audience. One way you can win people over is with this creamy Roasted Red Pepper Dip! Creative, eye-catching, and easy to make, this is a dip both you and your guests will happily devour. Feta cheese adds the perfect creamy element, along with those vital subtly sour notes Scorpios crave. If you don't have access to a grill, resourceful Scorpios can track down the roasted red peppers sold in a jar. Serve on a platter with choice of crostini, crackers, and a vegetable medley for dipping.

SERVES 8

2 large red bell peppers
1 medium hot banana pepper
1 scallion, ends trimmed
1 clove garlic
4 sun-dried tomatoes, packed in olive
   oil, drained and rinsed

1 cup crumbled feta cheese
1 cup coarsely chopped fresh basil
⅓ cup extra-virgin olive oil

1. Preheat a gas or charcoal grill to medium-high heat. Place all peppers on hot grill and char them on all sides. Place peppers in a bowl and cover tightly with plastic wrap. Cool 20 minutes. Remove charred skins and discard. Slit peppers in half; remove and discard seeds and stem.
2. Add peppers, scallion, garlic, tomatoes, feta, and basil to a food processor and pulse until smooth. With the processor running, slowly add oil. Serve at room temperature.

SPINACH AND FETA PIE

When it comes to entertaining, calculated Scorpio likes to bring a dish with intrigue. A pie is the perfect dish to spur curiosity. "What's in it?" they will wonder. But this time, your pie is a savory Spinach and Feta Pie! This Mediterranean specialty is filling, yet light, and packed with robust flavors that enchanting Scorpio adores. The oven does most of the work on this one, giving you more time to decide on how much black is appropriate to wear to this event. This pie is layered and complex like you, and everyone is going to want a slice, Scorpio, so maybe have some recipe cards ready to deflect any unwanted attention.

SERVES 8

- 1 bunch (about 4 cups) fresh spinach, stemmed
- 3 tablespoons olive oil
- 1 medium yellow onion, peeled and chopped
- 1 cup grated Swiss cheese
- 2 large eggs
- 1¼ cups light cream
- ½ teaspoon salt
- ¼ teaspoon ground black pepper
- ⅛ teaspoon ground nutmeg
- ¼ cup grated Parmesan cheese
- 1 (10") deep-dish pie crust, prebaked 5 minutes at 375°F
- 6 ounces feta cheese, crumbled
- 2 medium tomatoes, cored and sliced (optional)

1. Preheat oven to 350°F.
2. Steam spinach in a medium saucepan over medium heat until wilted, about 3–5 minutes. Squeeze out excess water and chop.
3. Heat olive oil in a small skillet over medium heat and cook onion until golden, about 7 minutes; toss with spinach. Stir in Swiss cheese.
4. In a blender, combine eggs, cream, salt, pepper, nutmeg, and Parmesan cheese. Blend 1 minute.
5. Spread spinach mixture into crust. Top with feta cheese and decorate with tomatoes if desired. Pour on the egg mixture, pressing through with your fingers to make sure it soaks through to the crust.
6. Bake 45 minutes until a knife inserted in the pie comes out clean. Serve hot or at room temperature.

TRIPLE CHOCOLATE CUPCAKES

You're often reserved, mysterious Scorpio, but one thing you're never shy about is your chocolate obsession. Get your chocolaty fix with these Triple Chocolate Cupcakes! Ambitious Scorpios know that when the chocolate cravings are this fierce, single or double chocolate just doesn't cut it. With so many varieties and qualities of chocolate available, driven Scorpios might like to try this recipe with an emphasis on milk chocolate, and again with dark chocolate—just to see which one you prefer!

--- **YIELDS 16 CUPCAKES** ---

4 ounces unsweetened chocolate squares
½ pound (2 sticks) unsalted butter
6 large eggs
1 cup granulated sugar
¾ cup cake flour

1½ teaspoons baking powder
2 teaspoons vanilla extract
1 tablespoon cocoa powder
⅛ teaspoon salt
1 cup mini chocolate morsels

1. Preheat oven to 350°F. Spray the cups of nonstick muffin tins with nonstick cooking spray.
2. In a small saucepan over low heat, melt chocolate and butter together. When melted, cool to room temperature.
3. Meanwhile, in a large mixing bowl, beat eggs with sugar until the mixture turns a pale lemon-yellow color. Spoon the cooled chocolate mixture into the egg mixture and stir until combined. Stir in cake flour, baking powder, vanilla, cocoa powder, and salt and beat for about 30 seconds. Stir in chocolate morsels. Spoon the mixture into the cups until each is about 2/3 full.
4. Bake 15–18 minutes or until a toothpick inserted in the center comes out clean and the cupcakes feel firm. Cool completely.

BLACKBERRY OATMEAL CRISP

This sensual dark fruit calls your name, Scorpio. Magnetic Scorpios cannot resist this baked Blackberry Oatmeal Crisp—especially while it's served warm, still fresh out of the oven! Oats are toasted to pleasurable perfection while the juicy berries burst and blend with the sugar and spices. Not too many desserts can be considered this nutritious, which is another bonus for you, sensual Scorpio. Double your taste bud bliss by pairing your oatmeal crisp with a scoop of vanilla ice cream, and you're in for a truly stellar treat!

SERVES 8

4 cups blackberries
⅓ cup granulated sugar
⅓ cup all-purpose flour
⅓ cup old-fashioned rolled oats
¼ cup unsalted butter, melted and
   cooled

¼ teaspoon ground cinnamon
¼ teaspoon ground lemon peel
¼ teaspoon ground nutmeg
¼ teaspoon ground ginger

1. Preheat oven to 350°F. Grease an 8" × 8" baking dish.
2. In a medium bowl, toss berries together with sugar. Pour into the bottom of prepared dish.
3. In a separate medium bowl, whisk together flour, oats, butter, and spices. Sprinkle over the berry mixture.
4. Bake 35 minutes or until the top is crisp and berries are bubbling. Let cool slightly before serving warm.

DARK 'N' STORMY

Committed Scorpios always have a preferred cocktail in which they'll routinely indulge. The Dark 'n' Stormy is that drink. Fizzy, refreshingly limey, and with a robust gingery kick, this drink arrives in a highball glass for even more sips. Enigmatic Scorpios adore the spike of ginger beer, but they especially love a spiked gingery mixed drink. Prepare to be enamored, dear Scorpio! Low-key enough for scorpions to sip all evening long, this delicious concoction is just the thing to help you relax and enjoy the storm.

SERVES 1

2 ounces Gosling's Black Seal rum
Ginger beer to fill

1 lime wedge

Pour rum over ice in a highball glass and fill with ginger beer. Squeeze in lime wedge.

Sagittarius:
The Innovator Chef

Bold Sagittarians are the life of the party! Warm and easygoing, these spirited fire signs have a fantastic sense of humor. They're engaging and jovial; when a Sagittarius speaks, we all listen—mostly because they are loud, but also because they are confident and hilarious. Ruled by Jupiter, planet of good luck, Sagittarians are risk-takers, and it often works out for them! Life is a gamble for fun-loving centaurs who live in the moment and fly by the seat of their pants. Sagittarius rules the hips in the body, and accordingly, these celestial centaurs are always on the move!

Expansive Jupiter gives Sagittarius a fierce hunger for life. As one of the more adventurous eaters of the zodiac, you'll try anything once! Thrill-seeking Sagittarians live large, whether collecting stamps on their passport or looking for the largest slices of pizza they can find. Time limits? Speed limits? Rules? Who needs 'em? Not you, Sagittarius, which is why you're the innovator chef! You're not afraid to change up the recipe on a whim purely because it sounds fun. Benevolent Sagittarians love cooking—especially with oversized cookware. The one thing you love more than hosting? Showing up at a party where you don't have to worry about cleaning up after.

HUEVOS RANCHEROS

You may be adventurous, dear Sag, but fortunately for you there's no need to travel far for this dish. "Huevos Rancheros" is Spanish for "rancher's eggs," and therefore perfect for celestial centaurs like you who delight in roaming wide-open pastures. Distinctively bold in flavor, this is a filling breakfast guaranteed to satisfy even the fiercest of hunger cravings. This recipe calls for eggs scrambled, but freedom-loving Sagittarians might like to try this with eggs sunny-side up. One more thing to make this dish pop? Sliced avocado for those days when you need a dose of extra fuel out on the range.

SERVES 4

1 (15-ounce) can Mexican-style black beans in sauce
2 cups salsa
8 large eggs
½ cup half-and-half
½ teaspoon salt

½ tablespoon unsalted butter
8 (8") soft corn tortillas
1 cup shredded Monterey jack or mild Cheddar cheese
½ cup sour cream
2 tablespoons chopped cilantro

1. Heat beans and salsa in separate small saucepans over low heat.
2. In a medium bowl, mix together eggs, half-and-half, and salt.
3. In a medium skillet over low heat, melt butter. Add the egg mixture and cook until soft and creamy, with small curds.
4. Soften tortillas either by steaming or flash cooking over an open gas burner. Place two tortillas on each plate. Divide black beans evenly onto tortillas. Spoon eggs onto the beans, then spoon salsa onto eggs. Garnish with cheese, sour cream, and cilantro. Serve immediately.

◦ ◦ ◦ ◦ FREEDOM TO CHOOSE ◦ ◦ ◦ ◦

You can certainly be extravagant, jovial Sagittarius, but sometimes you can't be bothered with extra effort. For this dish, feel free to use store-bought salsa, or better yet, buy fresh from a local Mexican grocery. Black beans are easy to prepare, but you're welcome to use a premade version here too.

APPLE CINNAMON YOGURT PANCAKES

Sagittarians are seekers of knowledge, though these restless adventurers much prefer hands-on experiences over stacks of books. Today, go for a stack of pancakes instead! Sagittarians adore fluffy pancakes, expertly browned, buttered, and drizzled in syrup. Yes, you do have a bit of a sweet tooth, dear Sag. These pancakes are made with high-protein yogurt, cinnamon, and apples, but feel free to swap out your apples with banana. The apple is long-held as a mythological symbol of knowledge. Will you find the knowledge you seek while eating these pancakes? Only one way to find out!

SERVES 4

1 large egg
1 cup plain yogurt
1 tablespoon canola oil
1 cup all-purpose flour
1 tablespoon granulated sugar

1 teaspoon baking powder
½ teaspoon baking soda
1 teaspoon ground cinnamon
⅛ teaspoon salt
½ cup thinly sliced apple pieces

1. In a blender, combine egg, yogurt, and oil until smooth.
2. In a medium bowl, sift flour, sugar, baking powder, baking soda, cinnamon, and salt together. Add to the yogurt mixture in blender and blend.
3. Prepare a hot griddle by spraying with nonstick cooking spray.
4. Ladle about ⅛ cup mixture onto the griddle.
5. Sprinkle each of the pancakes with apple pieces and cook until bubbles form in the pancake, about 3–4 minutes. Flip over and cook until done, about 1–2 minutes more. Serve.

∘ ∘ ∘ ∘ **BLENDER PANCAKES** ∘ ∘ ∘ ∘

Think your blender is only good for making smoothies and a mess? Think again! These superlight pancakes are supereasy to make in the blender. You can add the cinnamon to the ingredients or roll the apple slices in the cinnamon to coat them.

PUMPKIN PIE SMOOTHIE

Rabble-rousing Sagittarians are always down for a celebration. In fact, you were born during holiday season, which might be why your sign knows no limits when it comes to partying. With lovable warming spices that remind you of wintry desserts, this Pumpkin Pie Smoothie is just the thing for Sagittarian midday merriment. However, this smoothie is served cold, which means you can also enjoy it during the warmer months. You like options, celebratory Sag, so if fresh pumpkin cannot be found, canned works great too.

YIELDS 1½ CUPS

½ cup puréed fresh pumpkin
½ cup silken tofu
¼ cup dark brown sugar

1 cup skim milk
1 teaspoon pumpkin pie spice

---

1. Combine all the ingredients in a blender and purée until smooth.
2. Serve immediately.

○ ○ ○ ○ **TIME FLIES WHEN YOU'RE HAVING FUN** ○ ○ ○ ○

Characterized by a joie de vivre, Sagittarians are adept at losing track of time. They are professional procrastinators, and bedtime is often postponed in favor of spontaneous dance parties—because for these celestial centaurs, there is always a reason to celebrate! This time, make a toast to your health and sip this celebratory smoothie!

WHOLE-GRAIN PUMPKIN MUFFINS

Not surprisingly, these mutable fire signs are always on the move. While you like to travel light, dear Sagittarius, you'll definitely want to pack one of these muffins in your bag before you jet out the door. Packed with warming spices and energy-sustaining grains, these muffins are the perfect snack to help you maintain your gallop throughout the day. Pumpkin purée and Greek yogurt are what make these muffins unbelievably luscious and fluffy. Sagittarians can enjoy these satisfying muffins with almond butter or an afternoon coffee in between their daily activities. We can't always predict your next move, fiery Sag, but we do know that you will love this snack.

YIELDS 12 MUFFINS

1 large egg, beaten
1 cup puréed pumpkin
½ cup plain Greek yogurt
¼ cup canola oil
½ teaspoon ground cloves
½ teaspoon ground nutmeg
½ teaspoon allspice

½ teaspoon salt
1 teaspoon baking powder
1½ cups white whole-wheat flour
⅓ cup flaxseed meal
¼ cup old-fashioned rolled oats
⅓ cup whole pepitas
⅔ cup demerara sugar

1. Preheat oven to 350°F. Grease or line twelve wells in a muffin tin.
2. In a large bowl, stir together egg, pumpkin, yogurt, oil, cloves, nutmeg, allspice, and salt until smooth.
3. In a small bowl, whisk together the remaining ingredients. Add them to the pumpkin mixture and stir until just combined.
4. Divide the batter evenly among the wells in the muffin tin. Bake 15–20 minutes or until a toothpick inserted in the center of the center muffin comes out clean. Remove the muffins to a wire rack and cool completely.

CHEESE PIZZA

Multiple times, you have come close to proving that one truly can live off pizza alone. You sincerely believe that pizza deserves its own food group, and you'll make a solid case for yourself with this Cheese Pizza, persuasive Sag! The sky's the limit when it comes to toppings—an ideal situation for freedom-loving archers like you. Whimsical Sagittarians will delight in topping their pizza with literally anything they want. Feeling Hawaiian? Excellent. Plain? No worries. If you've never made your own dough before, you are in for a treat, celestial centaur. Get your hands in there and let the dough teach you all you need to know.

SERVES 10

DOUGH

4 cups all-purpose flour
½ teaspoon iodized salt
1–1⅓ cups cold water

PIZZA

1 cup pizza sauce
1 cup shredded provolone cheese
1 cup shredded mozzarella cheese
½ bulb garlic, minced
½ teaspoon dried oregano
½ teaspoon dried basil
½ teaspoon dried marjoram
½ teaspoon ground black pepper
½ tablespoon olive oil

1. Sift together flour and salt. Add to the bowl of a mixer and mix with water using a large dough hook for 3 minutes or until the ingredients are incorporated and the dough is formed. Let the dough rest 1 hour in the refrigerator.
2. Preheat oven to 425°F. Lightly grease two pizza pans with ½ tablespoon olive oil.
3. Roll out the dough on a floured surface into two large circles. Place the rolled dough on the pizza pans.
4. Ladle sauce over the dough, spreading it out evenly over the surface. Top with cheeses and sprinkle with garlic, herbs, and pepper. Drizzle with oil.
5. Bake 15–20 minutes until cheese is melted and the dough is cooked through. Let cool before slicing, then serve.

MANCHEGO AND POTATO TACOS WITH PICKLED JALAPEÑOS

If you aren't eating tacos, are you even living, Sagittarius? Philosophical Sagittarians love all tacos, but these fiery centaurs will especially adore these soft, cheesy potato tacos. Pickled jalapeños bring the heat, but you might also like to include the Mango Citrus Salsa (see recipe in this chapter) along with shredded purple cabbage for a complete taco experience. These tacos are lightly fried to offer hungry Sagittarians a crispier taco and also to melt the cheese into the potatoes. Yum! The stars are smiling on you, Sagittarius, because these tacos are out-of-this-world epic.

--- **SERVES 8** ---

1 cup leftover mashed potatoes
8 soft corn tortillas
¼ pound Spanish Manchego cheese
   or sharp Cheddar, cut into 16 small
   sticks

16 slices pickled jalapeño
4 tablespoons unsalted butter

1. Spoon 1 tablespoon mashed potato into the center of each tortilla. Flatten out potatoes, leaving a 1" border. Lay two pieces of cheese and two slices jalapeño onto each tortilla and fold closed into a half-moon shape.
2. In a large skillet over medium heat, melt 2 tablespoons butter. Gently lay four of the tacos into skillet and cook until nicely browned, about 3–4 minutes on each side.
3. Drain on paper towels. Repeat with remaining tacos. Serve.

COCONUT SHRIMP

Your philosophy is to enjoy life to the max, celebratory Sagittarius. Which is why you're serving up a crispy pan-fried favorite: Coconut Shrimp! With the perfect balance of spicy and sweet, and creamy and crisp, this dish has got your palate covered, Sagittarius. However, if you can't get enough of that coconut crunch, go ahead and sprinkle on some toasted coconut flakes at the very end.

SERVES 4

1 pound large shrimp, peeled and deveined
½ teaspoon salt
¼ cup coconut milk
2 tablespoons chicken broth
1 teaspoon palm sugar or brown sugar
1 teaspoon cornstarch
4 teaspoons water, or as needed

3 tablespoons vegetable or peanut oil, divided
½ teaspoon minced ginger
1 teaspoon minced garlic
¼ teaspoon chili paste with garlic
2 medium shallots, peeled and chopped
1 medium green bell pepper, seeded and cut into bite-sized cubes

1. Place shrimp in a medium bowl and toss with salt.
2. In a small bowl, combine coconut milk, chicken broth, and sugar. In a separate small bowl, dissolve cornstarch into 4 teaspoons water.
3. Heat a wok or medium skillet over medium-high heat until it is nearly smoking. Add 2 tablespoons oil. When oil is hot, add ginger and stir-fry 10 seconds. Add shrimp. Stir-fry shrimp until they turn pink, taking care not to overcook. Remove shrimp from pan and drain in a colander or on paper towels.
4. Heat remaining tablespoon oil in the wok or skillet. When oil is hot, add garlic and the chili paste. Stir-fry 10 seconds. Add shallots. Stir-fry shallots until softened, about 2 minutes, then add bell pepper. Stir-fry bell pepper 2 minutes or until it is tender but still crisp.
5. Push the vegetables to the sides of the pan. Add the coconut milk mixture in the middle and bring to a boil. Stir the cornstarch mixture and then pour into the coconut milk mixture, stirring to thicken. When sauce has thickened, add shrimp back into the pan. Stir-fry 1–2 more minutes to combine all the ingredients. Serve hot.

FRENCH ONION SOUP

As the celestial archer, you might shoot an arrow at a map to decide on your next vacation, but other times that arrow could be indicating your stomach's desires. This time, adventurous Sagittarius, you're aiming for French Onion Soup—an iconic French soup bursting with savory flavor and oozing with cheese. This version is made in a slow cooker, leaving you more time to browse for airline tickets. But for now, dear Sagittarius, let this bold yet comforting soup quell your endless wanderlust. Fill up your ramekins, top with toasted cheesy bread, and enjoy!

SERVES 8

1 tablespoon olive oil
5 medium onions, peeled and chopped
4 cloves garlic, minced
1 teaspoon granulated sugar
½ cup dry red wine
4 medium carrots, peeled and sliced
8 cups beef or mushroom stock
½ teaspoon salt

⅛ teaspoon ground black pepper
½ teaspoon dried marjoram leaves
1 (3-ounce) package cream cheese, softened
1 cup shredded Havarti cheese
2 tablespoons grated Parmesan cheese
1 medium baguette, sliced

1. In a 4- to 5-quart slow cooker, combine olive oil, onions, garlic, and sugar. Cover and cook on high 1–2 hours, stirring occasionally, until onions are a deep golden brown. Halfway through cooking time, add wine. Do not let this burn.
2. Add carrots, stock, salt, pepper, and marjoram. Cover and cook on low 4–5 hours.
3. Meanwhile, in a small bowl, combine cream cheese and Havarti and Parmesan cheeses.
4. Preheat broiler. Spread the cheese mixture on bread slices and broil until cheese begins to brown. Spoon soup into warm bowls and top with bread.

∘ ∘ ∘ ∘ TAKE A GAMBLE ∘ ∘ ∘ ∘

Thrill-seeking Sagittarians live in the moment, and they love taking risks. Of the signs, Sagittarius is voted the most likely to buy a scratch-off lottery ticket. Ruled by Jupiter, planet of abundance and good fortune, Lady Luck is often on these archers' sides.

MANGO CITRUS SALSA

This vibrant salsa is sure to pique your interest, Sagittarius. Spicy, sweet, and super-refreshing, this Mango Citrus Salsa is just the thing to brighten up Jerk Chicken and Coconut Shrimp, and if you really want to push the limits, why not add this sweet, tangy salsa to Huevos Rancheros (see recipes in this chapter)? You're unafraid to push the boundaries, Sag, so give it a whirl! No judgment here. You love making your own culinary discoveries, though we do have one tip for you: Firmer mangoes are easier to chop for this salsa, so save the juicier ones for later.

YIELDS 2 CUPS

1 large mango, peeled and chopped
2 medium tangerines, peeled and chopped
½ medium red bell pepper, seeded and chopped
½ medium red onion, peeled and minced

3 cloves garlic, minced
½ medium jalapeño, seeded and minced
2 tablespoons lime juice
½ teaspoon salt
¼ teaspoon ground black pepper
3 tablespoons chopped fresh cilantro

1. Gently toss together all the ingredients in a medium bowl.
2. Allow salsa to sit at least 15 minutes before serving to allow flavors to mingle.

∘ ∘ ∘ ∘ CHOP AND GO! ∘ ∘ ∘ ∘

Fiery Sagittarians are always on the move, so this is the perfect dish for you to take to your next party or barbecue. Simply chop everything up, toss it all in a bowl, and you are ready to go. What could be better for you, jovial Sagittarius, than to spend less time cooking and more time being the life of the party?

TROPICAL COBB SALAD

Life is a sunny beach for fun-loving Sagittarians, which is why you own at least seven pairs of sunglasses. So grab your favorite chaise lounge (and your favorite shades) because this summery salad is best enjoyed by a swimming pool. Indulgent Sagittarians prefer a hearty salad like a Cobb. Featuring juicy mango and grilled chicken, this Tropical Cobb Salad gets its crunch from toasted pine nuts. Yum! However, pleasure-seeking globe-trotters like you might also like to include your beloved salty bacon in this salad, and don't forget to choose a low-fat citrus dressing to serve on the side. There are no limits to this salad, freedom-loving Sag.

SERVES 1

2 cups romaine lettuce

3 ounces grilled chicken breast, sliced

¼ cup diced plum tomatoes

2 tablespoons chopped mangoes

½ tablespoon toasted pine nuts

1 tablespoon feta cheese

1 tablespoon sliced red onion

Combine all the ingredients in a medium bowl and serve.

∘ ∘ ∘ ∘ DRESS TO IMPRESS ∘ ∘ ∘ ∘

You'll want a citrusy salad dressing to showcase the sweetness of the mango in this salad. Fortunately, you can always make your own by whisking together lime juice, olive oil, crushed garlic, and a pinch of sugar, salt, and pepper. Easy. And you like easy, breezy Sagittarius.

JERK CHICKEN

Outspoken Sagittarians tell it like it is. These fun-loving centaurs never mean to offend, but sometimes their boldness comes on a bit strong. But lucky for you, opinionated Sag, there's never a need to tone it down in the kitchen! You crave a dish as bold and fiery as you, so you go with none other than Jerk Chicken! Like you, the fierce spices showcased in this dish do not hold back. Scotch bonnet peppers are hot, but risk-taking centaurs always delight in the distinctive heat of Jamaican jerk spice. Vegetarian archers can try this recipe with pressed tofu. Serve with fresh basmati rice, sweet plantains, and the Mango Citrus Salsa (see recipe in this chapter) for a meal as vibrant as you!

SERVES 8

8 whole chicken leg quarters
⅓ cup canola oil
⅓ cup lime juice
¼ cup light brown sugar
3 tablespoons apple cider vinegar
1½ tablespoons fresh thyme leaves
3 teaspoons allspice
½ teaspoon mace
1 teaspoon ground black pepper

1½ teaspoons sea salt
1 teaspoon ground cinnamon
½ teaspoon ground cloves
¼ teaspoon freshly ground nutmeg
1 bunch scallions, ends trimmed
6 cloves garlic
1 small onion, peeled and quartered
6 Scotch bonnet peppers
1 (1") knob ginger, sliced

1. Place chicken in a marinating container or resealable plastic bag. Set aside. Place the remaining ingredients in a blender or food processor and pulse until smooth. Pour over chicken. Refrigerate chicken 8–12 hours.
2. Prepare your charcoal grill according to manufacturer's instructions. Grill the chicken over high, direct heat until the skin begins to caramelize.
3. Reduce the heat and continue to cook, covered, until chicken is fully cooked, about 30–40 minutes. If desired, use the remaining marinade to baste the chicken during the cooking process. (Be sure to adequately cook any extra marinade that may have touched the uncooked chicken.) Serve immediately.

BEEF MEATBALLS

You like to go big or go home, Sagittarius, so here's the meatball recipe you need to knock dinner out of the park. Laid-back Sagittarians are always down for dishes that are simple and yet extraordinary in taste, and meatballs are an excellent way to achieve these goals. Garlic and Parmesan cheese give these meatballs a bold flavor appreciated by boisterous Sagittarians everywhere. This recipe is simple and to the point (you always appreciate directness, Sag), leaving embellishments up to you! Freedom-loving Sagittarians can serve these over angel hair pasta or toast up some rolls and make meatball subs.

SERVES 10

5 thick slices day-old or toasted Italian bread
½ bulb garlic, minced
¼ bunch fresh parsley, chopped
1½ pounds lean ground beef

1 large egg, lightly beaten
¼ cup fresh-grated Parmesan or Romano cheese
½ teaspoon ground black pepper

1. Soak bread in water 1 minute. Thoroughly squeeze out all the liquid.
2. In a large mixing bowl, combine all the ingredients. Form the mixture into balls about 2"–3" in size.
3. To bake the meatballs: Preheat oven to 375°F. Place the meatballs in a lightly greased baking pan and cover. Bake 30 minutes. Uncover and brown 5–10 minutes.
4. To fry the meatballs: Heat about 1 tablespoon olive oil over medium heat in a large skillet. Fry meatballs 30 minutes, uncovered, stirring occasionally until cooked through.
5. Transfer the meatballs to paper towels to drain and serve as you desire.

WHITE BEAN ARTICHOKE DIP

Sagittarians are fantastic hosts, but they much prefer showing up to the party as guests. Known for their grand entrances and distinctive generosity, Sagittarians never show up empty-handed. This lovable dip is huge on flavor, easy to make, and even easier to transport. It might be hard to believe a dip this delicious could be so healthy. Believe it, Sag. Serve with pita triangles and a medley of vegetables for dipping options everyone can get excited about.

SERVES 20

1 pound cooked cannellini beans
14 ounces fresh or defrosted frozen
    artichoke hearts
2 cloves garlic, minced

1 tablespoon plain Greek yogurt
¼ cup lemon juice
¼ cup feta cheese
2 tablespoons minced fresh dill

1. Place all the ingredients in a food processor. Pulse until slightly chunky.
2. To serve cold: Refrigerate 1 hour prior to serving.
3. To serve warm: Preheat oven to 350°F. Grease a small casserole pan and pour dip into it. Bake 15 minutes or until warmed through. Serve immediately.

LETTUCE-WRAPPED TURKEY WITH CRANBERRY MAYONNAISE AND APPLES

Jovial Sagittarians are always the life of the party—but you can bring even more pizazz to the party with these vivacious deli wraps. Sagittarians have a low-key obsession with horseradish. Is it because centaurs are part horse? Or is it because of their fiery constitution? Either way, spicy horseradish pairs perfectly with turkey, and it bridges the sweetness of the cranberry and the creaminess of the mayonnaise into an irresistible flavor combo. Easygoing Sagittarians can never pass up a handheld party snack— especially one with this much freshness and outstanding texture.

SERVES 1

2 large romaine lettuce leaves
¼ pound deli turkey, diced
2 teaspoons low-fat mayonnaise
1 teaspoon jelled cranberry sauce
1 teaspoon prepared horseradish
½ medium stalk celery, chopped fine

1 slice onion, chopped fine
½ medium tart apple, cored and chopped fine
1 tablespoon toasted and chopped walnuts

1. Lay lettuce leaves on a work surface. Place diced turkey on top of the lettuce leaves.
2. In a small bowl, mix together mayonnaise, cranberry sauce, and horseradish.
3. Mix celery, onion, apple, and walnuts with the mayonnaise mixture. Spread on the turkey and roll up the wrap.

∘ ∘ ∘ ∘ IT'S A WRAP! ∘ ∘ ∘ ∘

Breezy Sagittarians are excellent innovators, so when you have a lot of people to serve, forgo the lettuce wraps in favor of giant deli wraps. Place toothpicks about 1"–1½" apart down the middle of your finished wrap and slice between them. This keeps your wrap intact as you slice and, voilà! Perfect party hors d'oeuvres!

CINNAMON ROLLS

Celebratory Sagittarians stride boldly toward all the sweetness in life. So these celestial centaurs will find themselves gliding toward an irresistibly fluffy batch of these Cinnamon Rolls hot out of the oven. Every Sagittarius has a sweet spot in their heart (and room in their stomach) for a sticky cinnamon roll. These pastries are an ideal breakfast treat for jovial Sagittarians and perfect for parties.

SERVES 10

DOUGH

1 (0.25-ounce) packet dry active yeast
½ cup warm water
3 cups all-purpose flour
¼ cup brown sugar
⅛ teaspoon iodized salt
3 large eggs
1 cup scalded milk (cooled thoroughly)

FILLING

1 cup melted unsalted butter
3 tablespoons ground cinnamon
½ cup granulated sugar

FROSTING

1 cup confectioners' sugar
1 teaspoon vanilla extract
1½ cups whole milk

1. In a small bowl, stir yeast into water. Let stand 3–5 minutes until frothy.
2. In a large bowl, sift together flour, sugar, and salt.
3. In a small bowl, mix together eggs and cooled milk.
4. Add the yeast mixture and egg mixture to the flour mixture and combine and mix until a ball forms. Add the dough to a greased bowl and allow it to rest 1 hour in a warm place.
5. While the dough rests, combine all the filling ingredients in a small bowl.
6. Mix together all the frosting ingredients in a medium bowl. Store the frosting in the refrigerator until ready to use.
7. Preheat oven to 375°F. Grease a sheet pan.
8. Punch down the dough once it has doubled in size. On a floured surface, roll it out into a ½"-thick rectangle. Paint the dough with the filling mixture and roll it up into a log. Cut the log into 3" sections. Place on prepared pan.
9. Bake 45 minutes until brown. Let cool slightly and then frost. Serve.

GINGERBREAD CARROT CAKE

Innovative Sagittarians will appreciate the unique addition of crystalized ginger in this carrot cake. Featuring all the mellow, warming spices that exuberant Sagittarius adores, this Gingerbread Carrot Cake pairs exquisitely with the sweet Cream Cheese Frosting. This is a fabulous cake that lively Sagittarians can enjoy during winter celebrations. Celestial centaurs are always down for merriment and revelry, so put this one on a platter and convince everyone to join you.

SERVES 20

CAKE

1 (16-ounce) package baby carrots
¼ cup chopped crystallized ginger
1 cup granulated sugar
1 cup brown sugar
½ cup honey
¾ cup vegetable oil
2 large eggs
4 large egg whites
⅔ cup orange juice
1 tablespoon ground ginger
1 teaspoon ground cinnamon
½ teaspoon ground cloves

½ teaspoon salt
1½ cups all-purpose flour
1½ cups whole-wheat pastry flour
2 teaspoons baking powder
½ teaspoon baking soda

CREAM CHEESE FROSTING

2 tablespoons butter, softened
3 (3-ounce) packages cream cheese, softened
⅓ cup sour cream
4 cups confectioners' sugar
2 teaspoons vanilla extract
⅛ teaspoon salt

1. Preheat oven to 350°F. Spray a 13" × 9" pan with nonstick baking spray containing flour and set aside.
2. Place carrots in a food processor. Process until finely ground; remove half of the carrots to a large bowl. Add crystallized ginger to food processor; process until finely ground. Add to large bowl.

3. Add granulated sugar, brown sugar, honey, oil, eggs, egg whites, and orange juice and mix well. Stir in ground ginger, cinnamon, cloves, salt, flours, baking powder, and baking soda and stir until combined. Spread in prepared pan.
4. Bake 45–55 minutes or until cake is dark golden brown and begins to pull away from the sides of pan. Cool completely on a wire rack.
5. In a large bowl, combine butter, cream cheese, and sour cream; beat well until fluffy. Add half of the confectioners' sugar; beat until fluffy. Stir in vanilla and salt and beat well. Add remaining confectioners' sugar, beating constantly until frosting reaches desired spreading consistency.
6. Spread cooled cake with the frosting. Store leftovers covered at room temperature.

○ ○ ○ ○ **FABULOUS FROSTING!** ○ ○ ○ ○

Inventive Sagittarians will love the versatility of this frosting since you can flavor it in many different ways. This frosting, even though it has cream cheese and sour cream, can be transformed into a chocolate frosting by beating in 2 ounces of melted unsweetened chocolate. Or create a caramel frosting by stirring in 1/2 cup caramel ice cream topping. All the delicious possibilities are sure to hit your sweet tooth in all the right places, Sagittarius!

MINT JULEP

Rabble-rousing Sagittarians love bourbon, so your celestial cocktail hails from the Kentucky Bourbon Trail. The mint julep is the signature drink of the Kentucky Derby. Jovial centaurs will be quick out of the gate as they gallop toward their home bar to mix this minty muddled spirit. With a touch of sugar to sweeten the pot, odds are that the green-hued Mint Julep will become a favorite of fiery Sagittarians. Sip this beautiful concoction, dear Sag, and you'll surely feel like luck is on your side.

SERVES 1
---

5 sprigs spearmint leaves, divided
1 tablespoon granulated sugar

Crushed ice
2 ounces bourbon

1. Muddle four spearmint sprigs and sugar in a highball glass. Fill with ice. Add bourbon and stir until glass gets very cold.
2. Add more ice if needed. Garnish with remaining spearmint sprig.

Capricorn:
The Sophisticated Chef

Capricorns are represented by the mythological sea goat. With an innate capability to climb the highest mountain peaks, but also dive deep to the lowest depths of the ocean, these practical earth signs channel their emotions into something tangible. Yes, these stellar sea goats are notorious for their ambition. Ruled by Saturn, lord of time, Capricorns are not impulsive risk-takers, but rather are methodical and calculated achievers. With the long term in mind, Capricorns are patient. They understand that the best things in life are worth waiting for. An important goal for ambitious Capricorns? Cushy retirement. Capricorns can be realistic to a fault, but they only work hard so that they can play hard! Once the day is done, Capricorns are ready to get lit!

Sophisticated and put together, Capricorns tend to have fine taste. Less is more for these refined earth signs. These classy minimalists value quality over quantity—which is also evident in their cooking style! In the kitchen, classy Capricorns aim to impress with simple plates elevated with mastery. No frills needed. Elegant and playful Capricorns know a thing or two about good timing, so have a seat at their table and watch them pull out all the stops!

HOMEMADE BREAKFAST SAUSAGE PATTIES

Capricorns require a solid breakfast, so these celestial sea goats will delight in preparing their own sausage—a tried-and-true breakfast standby. Homemade? Sounds impressive, and yet, it's supereasy. Ambitious Capricorns love excelling with minimal effort. In fact, one of Capricorn's mottos is "work smarter, not harder." Capricorns have high standards of quality, and it doesn't get fresher than homemade! Ruled by Saturn, Capricorns gravitate toward bitter herbs like fennel and sage, which characterize sausage's signature taste. Sausage ingredients are prepared the night prior, making mornings even easier for efficient Capricorn. Serve with eggs and toast for a complete breakfast!

SERVES 6

1 pound lean ground pork
1 medium shallot, peeled and grated
1 clove garlic, grated
2 teaspoons ground sage
1 teaspoon red pepper flakes
1 teaspoon light brown sugar
½ teaspoon paprika

½ teaspoon fennel seed
¼ teaspoon ground rosemary
¼ teaspoon ground white pepper
¼ teaspoon ground mustard
¼ teaspoon kosher salt
⅛ teaspoon allspice
⅛ teaspoon ground cloves

1. Place all the ingredients in a medium bowl and stir to thoroughly combine. Cover and refrigerate overnight.
2. Measure out ¼ cup mixture and form into a flat patty. Repeat until the mixture is gone.
3. Cook in a medium nonstick skillet over medium heat until brown on all sides and fully cooked, about 4–6 minutes per side. Serve.

SHAKSHUKA

Sophisticated Capricorns will adore Shakshuka, a popular tomato-based North African eggy dish bursting with flavor. This dish features harissa, an earthy spice paste that is often used in soups, marinades, spreads, and much more. Adventurous Capricorns can make their own harissa, or this increasingly popular paste can also be purchased premade. Enjoy Shakshuka on its own, with pita bread, or, for the overachievers, with thick cuts of grilled bread. Packed with protein and vegetables, this flavorful breakfast is one that checks all the boxes for you, prestigious Capricorn!

SERVES 6

- 3 tablespoons olive oil
- 4 cloves garlic, minced
- 3 medium jalapeños, seeded and minced
- 1 large shallot, peeled and minced
- 28 ounces canned crushed or ground tomatoes
- 1 tablespoon harissa
- ¼ teaspoon salt
- ½ teaspoon ground black pepper
- ½ teaspoon roasted ground cumin
- 6 large eggs
- 1½ tablespoons minced fresh Italian parsley

1. Heat oil in a 12" cast-iron skillet over medium heat. Add garlic, jalapeños, and shallot and sauté until fragrant and golden, about 5–10 minutes.
2. Add tomatoes, harissa, salt, pepper, and cumin and stir. Simmer until tomatoes reduce slightly and are warmed through, about 10 minutes.
3. Crack eggs into the pan, forming a single layer of egg on top of the tomato mixture. Cook until the yolks are barely set and the whites are fully cooked, about 5 minutes. Sprinkle with parsley. Serve immediately.

GREEN TEA SMOOTHIE

You're no slacker, Capricorn, so when that midday slump catches up with you, a little caffeine is just the thing to perk you up again. Consistent Capricorns will appreciate an energizing smoothie like this one to help them maintain a steady pace as they power through their remaining tasks for the day. Fresh fruits team up with green tea for an antioxidant-rich smoothie that isn't overly sweet. This energy-sustaining smoothie is the perfect midday drink to offer Capricorn immediate health results—while also supplying long-term antiaging benefits as well.

YIELDS 2½ CUPS (SERVES 2)

1 medium frozen banana, peeled and chopped
6 frozen strawberries
1 medium kiwi, peeled

2½ tablespoons raw honey
2 cups green tea
½ cup ice

1. Combine all the ingredients in a blender and process until smooth.
2. Serve immediately.

○ ○ ○ ○ TIMELESS CAPRICORN ○ ○ ○ ○

Ruled by protective and supportive Saturn, Capricorn governs the skin and skeletal structures in the body. Capricorns tend to have good skin genetically, but also because they frequently invest in antiaging products. Antioxidants like green tea are astronomically appealing to Capricorns—the zodiac sign who is rumored to get younger with age.

GNOCCHI AND PURPLE POTATOES WITH BROCCOLINI

Capricorn, you're known to be a purist at heart. Which is why you can never go wrong with dumplings! Nearly every culture has its own version of dumpling, but today, you're going with the sumptuous Italian dumpling, gnocchi! Classy Capricorns might like to buy it handmade from the farmers' market, while driven Capricorns might like to make their own! For added texture, you can crisp the purple potatoes in the oven on high about 25 minutes, add the Broccolini, and then roast an additional 15 minutes. Overall this is a highly balanced, healthy meal boasting acidic, herbal, and umami flavor profiles—guaranteed to satisfy your palate, elegant Capricorn!

SERVES 4

1 (17.6-ounce) package fresh gnocchi
1 bunch Broccolini, chopped and cooked
10 baby purple potatoes, cooked and cubed
1 (13.75-ounce) can artichoke hearts, drained and quartered

3 tablespoons capers
½ cup olive oil
3 tablespoons red wine vinegar
2 tablespoons pesto
⅛ teaspoon salt
⅛ teaspoon ground black pepper

1. Cook gnocchi according to package directions, drain, and put into a serving bowl. Add Broccolini, potatoes, artichoke hearts, and capers.
2. In a small bowl, whisk together oil, vinegar, pesto, salt, and pepper.
3. Pour the oil mixture over the vegetables and toss to combine. Serve.

○ ○ ○ ○ **MULTIPURPOSE POTATOES** ○ ○ ○ ○

Efficient Capricorns are always seeking to discover new ways to use their favorite ingredients, which is one reason why Capricorns love potatoes! This recipe features potatoes two different ways: Gnocchi is made with mashed potatoes, egg, and flour, while the purple potatoes are open to interpretation.

ROAST BEEF WITH CARAMELIZED ONION PANINI

Down-to-earth Capricorns appreciate simplicity and straightforwardness, and yet they tend to be difficult to impress. Here is a flavorful handheld lunch that is sure to wow this celestial sea goat! That's right, the panini press does all the work for you (even caramelizing the onions and mushrooms!), leaving one fewer pan to clean up. Roast beef is easily one of the most flavorful of deli meats, and therefore, one of your favorites, luxurious Capricorn! Easy, delicious, and fast cleanup—everything you ever want in a sandwich, Capricorn!

SERVES 1

1 tablespoon olive oil
1 small yellow onion, peeled and sliced
¼ cup sliced mushrooms
1 teaspoon garlic powder
¼ teaspoon salt, divided

¼ teaspoon ground black pepper, divided
1 long roll or baguette
⅛–¼ pound roast beef, sliced

---

1. Preheat the panini press. In a small bowl, add olive oil, onion, mushrooms, garlic powder, ⅛ teaspoon salt, and ⅛ teaspoon pepper and mix to coat the ingredients with oil. Empty the bowl onto the heated press and drizzle additional olive oil on top as desired. Close the press and cook 4–5 minutes. After 3 minutes, you may open the press and mix the ingredients with a wooden spoon to ensure that they are evenly cooked. Remove them from the press and set aside.

2. Place the bottom half of the roll or baguette on the counter and add roast beef onto bread. Sprinkle with remaining salt and pepper and top with the onion mixture.

3. Add the top of the roll or baguette and place the sandwich on the press. Close the press and cook 3–5 minutes.

4. Remove the panini, slice in half, and serve warm.

CHEESY TOMATO BRUSCHETTA

Capricorns crave a quick and easy snack like bruschetta. This Cheesy Tomato Bruschetta is classically cheesy and garlicky and guaranteed to hit the spot for straightforward sea goats. And the best part? This snack takes only 10 minutes to make! Bruschetta is the perfect go-to snack when you get home from work. Cheesy and toasty bruschetta pairs perfectly with white wine, making this snack an ideal option for happy-hour noshes at your place. You love when a recipe has multiple purposes, Capricorn, so try the tomato mixture from this one as a marinade or mix with a spoonful of hummus to make yet another tasty dip.

SERVES 10

¼ cup tomato paste
2 tablespoons olive oil
1 (14-ounce) can diced Italian
   tomatoes, drained

3 cloves garlic, minced
1 teaspoon dried basil leaves
1 cup grated Parmesan cheese
16 (½") slices Italian bread

1. Preheat broiler in oven; set oven rack 6" from heat source.
2. In a medium bowl, combine tomato paste and olive oil; blend well until smooth. Add the remaining ingredients except for bread and mix gently.
3. Place bread slices on broiler pan. Broil bread slices until golden on one side, about 1–3 minutes. Turn and broil until light golden brown on second side. Remove from oven and top with the tomato mixture. Return to oven and broil 3–5 minutes or until tomato topping is bubbly and begins to brown. Serve immediately.

ROASTED BRUSSELS SPROUTS WITH APPLES

Capricorns are considered old souls, so chances are, you've never had a bad relationship with vegetables. However, if that's not the case between you and Brussels sprouts, this recipe is sure to change your mind! Balsamic vinegar is the ideal companion to Brussels sprouts, as it softens and adds a lovable tart dimension to this notorious cruciferous vegetable. And since you're always looking to take things to the next level, ambitious Capricorn, go ahead and top your dish with Brie for the final 5 minutes. Yes, this is one classy vegetable dish fit for a reputable sea goat such as yourself!

SERVES 4

---

2 cups Brussels sprouts, chopped into quarters
8 whole cloves garlic, peeled
2 tablespoons olive oil

2 tablespoons balsamic vinegar
¾ teaspoon salt
½ teaspoon ground black pepper
2 medium apples, cored and chopped

---

1. Preheat oven to 425°F.
2. Arrange Brussels sprouts and garlic in a single layer on a baking sheet. Drizzle with oil and vinegar and season with salt and pepper. Roast 10–12 minutes, tossing once.
3. Remove sheet from oven and add apples, tossing gently to combine. Roast 10 more minutes or until apples are soft, tossing once again. Serve.

ROASTED BAY SCALLOPS WITH SWISS CHARD

Calculated Capricorns won't pursue a feat unless there's a surefire guarantee that they can land it. Leave it to these cultivated sea goats to masterfully prepare scallops—an upscale dish that is fast and easy to make, and yet requires a certain level of finesse to perfect (careful not to over- or undercook these buttery sea creatures!). Prestigious Capricorns will adore the bright notes of citrus and garlic, which elevate the gentle sweetness of the scallops. However, it's the delicate panko coating that adds the perfect crispiness to this dish that Capricorn cannot resist.

SERVES 4

1½ pounds bay scallops
¾ cup chopped steamed Swiss chard
⅓ cup seafood stock
2 tablespoons lemon juice
½ tablespoon lemon zest
2 cloves garlic, minced
1 small onion, peeled and minced
1 tablespoon minced fresh Italian
 parsley

¼ teaspoon sea salt
¾ cup panko
1 teaspoon minced fresh basil
1 medium shallot, peeled and minced
¼ teaspoon ground black pepper
¼ teaspoon celery seed

---

1. Preheat oven to 350°F.
2. In a medium bowl, combine scallops, Swiss chard, stock, lemon juice, lemon zest, garlic, onion, parsley, and salt. Pour into an oiled 1½-quart baking dish. Use the back of a spoon to spread the mixture into a smooth, even layer.
3. In a small bowl, whisk together panko, basil, shallot, pepper, and celery seed. Sprinkle over the scallop mixture.
4. Bake 30 minutes or until scallops are just cooked through and panko is golden. Serve.

VICHYSSOISE
(Potato and Leek Soup)

Capricorn, your reputation for being serious is well founded, but certain things are guaranteed to get you to turn a smile. Try saying "Vichyssoise" without giggling: vish-ee-swah! Superfun to say and sophisticated at the same time! This simple puréed French soup will appeal to down-to-earth Capricorns everywhere, whether it's a low-key evening at home or part of a fancy four-course dinner. Potatoes create the creaminess of this soup, while herbs, leeks, and white wine build the iconic mellow flavor profile that all Capricorns will adore.

SERVES 12

1 tablespoon olive oil
1 medium onion, peeled and chopped
1 pound (about 3–4) potatoes, any
    variety, peeled and cut into 1" chunks
2 bunches leeks, trimmed and
    chopped, 1 cup reserved for garnish

1 teaspoon dried sage leaves
1 bay leaf
¼ cup white wine
2 quarts vegetable stock
⅛ teaspoon salt
⅛ teaspoon ground white pepper

1. In a large soup pot over medium heat, heat oil 1 minute. Add onion, potatoes, and all but 1 cup chopped leeks. Cook 10 minutes until onions turn translucent.
2. Add sage, bay leaf, and wine. Cook 1 minute more. Add stock. Bring to a full boil; reduce heat to a simmer and cook 45 minutes until potatoes are very tender and starting to fall apart.
3. Discard bay leaf, then carefully purée the soup in a blender in small batches. Season with salt and pepper.
4. Steam, boil, or sauté remaining cup of leeks, and serve the soup garnished with a spoonful of leeks in the center of each bowl.

WILTED KALE SALAD WITH ROASTED SHALLOTS

Capricorn, you appreciate honesty, so we are going to give you the truth straight up: Kale is one of the most nutritious greens you can eat. High in calcium and loaded with antioxidants, this reliable green is ideal for focused Capricorns. If you're from the northern hemisphere, Capricorn, you were born during the cold winter—a time when most salads lose their appeal. However, this satisfying salad is sure to tempt your taste buds even when the temperature drops! Want to make this salad even cozier? Add a sprinkle of cinnamon to add a mellow spicy element. Leave it to you to take things to the next level of tasty, Capricorn!

SERVES 10

10 cups peeled whole medium shallots
⅓ cup olive oil
3 large bunches kale

2 tablespoons balsamic vinegar
½ teaspoon coarse salt
½ teaspoon ground black pepper

---

1. Preheat oven to 375°F.
2. In a large bowl, toss shallots in oil. Place on a roasting pan and roast until fork-tender, about 20 minutes. Remove from oven and slice shallots in half.
3. While shallots roast, quickly wilt kale in boiling water for 1 minute. Remove from heat, drain, and set aside to cool.
4. Serve by mounding cooked kale in the center of a plate or platter. Top with shallots, drizzle with vinegar, and sprinkle with salt and pepper.

○ ○ ○ ○ LOVE, YOUR FRIEND, KALE ○ ○ ○ ○

Since Capricorn rules the skeletal system in the body, all realistic Capricorns can get down with this calcium-rich leafy green. You might not love it all the time, but you'll make a point to eat it on the regular. Fortunately for you, dear Capricorn, this is one recipe in which kale is undeniably delicious.

GREEK-STYLE FLANK STEAK

Ambitious Capricorns work hard for one reason: the rewards! That's why you're eating flank steak for dinner. High-quality, time-tested, and guaranteed to satisfy, this is the expertly char-marked dish elegant Capricorns crave at the end of their day. Don't want to grill? No problem. Flank steak can also be prepared in a skillet. But we'll let you call the shots, executive Capricorn! Pair with the Vichyssoise, Roasted Brussels Sprouts with Apples, or Wilted Kale Salad with Roasted Shallots (see recipes in this chapter) for a complete dinner that meets your sophisticated standards.

SERVES 8

¼ cup extra-virgin olive oil
8 cloves garlic, smashed
4 medium scallions, chopped and
  ends trimmed
1 tablespoon Dijon mustard
⅓ cup balsamic vinegar
2 tablespoons fresh thyme leaves

2 tablespoons fresh rosemary leaves
1 teaspoon dried oregano
1½ teaspoons salt, divided
¾ teaspoon ground black pepper,
  divided
1 (2-pound) flank steak
3 tablespoons vegetable oil

1. In a food processor, process olive oil, garlic, scallions, mustard, vinegar, thyme, rosemary, oregano, 1 teaspoon salt, and ½ teaspoon pepper until incorporated.
2. Rub steak with the marinade and place in a medium baking dish. Cover and refrigerate 3 hours.
3. Return steak to room temperature before grilling. Wipe most of the marinade off steak and season with remaining salt and pepper.
4. Preheat a gas or charcoal grill to medium-high. Brush grill surface to make sure it is thoroughly clean. When grill is ready, dip a clean tea towel in vegetable oil and wipe the grill surface with oil. Place meat on the grill and grill 4 minutes per side.
5. Let steak rest 5 minutes before serving.

GRILLED PORTOBELLO MUSHROOMS

Earthy Capricorn, you're a no-frills kind of sea goat. You'd rather let the ingredients speak for themselves, which is why you'll find that these Grilled Portobello Mushrooms are straightforwardly delicious. You're happy to enjoy them perfectly as is, or, as a cardinal sign, you're known to take calculated risks (note: calculated). So fortunately for you, clever Capricorn, whatever embellishments you apply to your portobellos is up to your culinary expertise. Stuff and bake to your liking or serve up with pearled couscous. You're full of good ideas, confident Capricorn, so we'll trust you to lead the way!

SERVES 6

6 portobello mushrooms
2 tablespoons olive oil
2 cloves garlic, minced

1 teaspoon salt
½ teaspoon ground black pepper

---

1. Preheat a gas or charcoal grill to medium-high heat.
2. Clean off the mushrooms with damp paper towels or a mushroom brush and scrape out the black membrane on the underside of the cap.
3. Mix oil and garlic together in a shallow dish. Dip each mushroom in the dish and place on a rack to drain.
4. Season with salt and pepper.
5. Grill 5 minutes per side until fork-tender. Serve mushrooms whole or sliced.

∘ ∘ ∘ ∘ FUN ON A BUN ∘ ∘ ∘ ∘

You want the finer things in life, Capricorn, so at your next party serve up your favorite fungi on a bun! For an out-of-this-world mushroom burger your guests will rave about, add chimichurri, roasted red peppers, a slice of red onion, fresh arugula, and a slathering of aioli. Astronomically delicious!

TURKEY PICCATA

Elegant Capricorn is the host with the most. Capricorn likes to host formal gatherings so that they have an excuse to finally utilize those fancy plates that they have inherited. So the next time you're hosting dinner for ten people, you can't go wrong with Turkey Piccata! Capricorns adore lemony, lightly breaded piccata cutlets with briny bursts of capers—and undoubtedly, so will your guests! This recipe uses olive oil, but if you desire that iconic buttery flavor, substitute a tablespoon of olive oil with butter. Just don't forget the candelabras and silk napkins, fancy Capricorn!

SERVES 10

3–4 pounds boneless turkey breast
2 tablespoons olive oil
½ cup all-purpose flour
2 tablespoons capers, rinsed

Zest and juice of 2 large lemons
1 cup chicken stock
½ bunch fresh parsley, chopped
½ teaspoon ground black pepper

1. Slice turkey into serving-sized portions.
2. In a large sauté pan, heat oil over medium heat. Dust turkey with flour and shake off excess. Add turkey to pan and brown the turkey pieces on one side, then turn.
3. Add capers, lemon zest and juice, and stock. Cook 6–10 minutes longer until browned and cooked through.
4. Sprinkle with parsley and pepper and serve.

GREEK PIZZA

Fancy parties might be your forte, Capricorn, but you also know how to keep it real with a homemade pizza. Make that a Greek Pizza! Down-to-earth Capricorns will adore the gremolata topping on this pizza. What's gremolata? It's the vibrant trifecta of parsley, lemon zest, and minced garlic. All flavors you love, Capricorn. Toppings are open to your expert interpretation, Capricorn—and that's a good thing, because you like calling the shots! Look forward to serving this crowd-pleasing pizza at a casual Sunday gathering or as a late-night party snack!

SERVES 6

1 tablespoon olive oil
1 medium onion, peeled and chopped
5 cloves garlic, minced, divided
2 medium green bell peppers, seeded and chopped
2 medium tomatoes, cored and chopped
¼ cup tomato paste
2 tablespoons lemon juice

¼ teaspoon salt
⅛ teaspoon cayenne pepper
1 teaspoon dried oregano
1 prebaked pizza crust
1 cup shredded part-skim mozzarella cheese
¼ cup crumbled feta cheese
¼ cup minced parsley
2 teaspoons grated lemon zest

1. Preheat oven to 400°F.
2. In a large skillet, heat olive oil over medium heat. Add onion and 3 cloves garlic; cook and stir until crisp-tender, about 5 minutes. Add bell peppers, tomatoes, tomato paste, lemon juice, salt, cayenne pepper, and oregano and bring to a simmer. Simmer 5 minutes, stirring frequently.
3. Place crust on a cookie sheet. Spread the tomato mixture over crust and top with mozzarella and feta cheeses. Bake 20–25 minutes or until crust is very crisp and cheeses are melted and begin to brown.
4. In a small bowl, combine parsley, lemon zest, and remaining 2 cloves garlic and mix well. Sprinkle over the pizza and serve immediately.

SUGAR COOKIES

Cultivated Capricorns don't always indulge in dessert, but when they do, you can bet they'll go for a cookie. This time, you're going with Sugar Cookies—straightforwardly sweet, this simple cookie is here to satisfy the celestial sea goat in a big way. Pure and simple, dessert really doesn't get any better than this. And the best part? You already have all these ingredients at home and can make these cookies in just 15 minutes. For someone who doesn't like to wait around, Sugar Cookies are your ideal dessert!

YIELDS 20 COOKIES

1 cup all-purpose flour
½ cup whole-wheat flour
¾ cup granulated sugar
¼ teaspoon salt
1 teaspoon baking powder

3 tablespoons canola oil
1 large egg
2 tablespoons skim milk
2 teaspoons vanilla extract

1. Preheat oven to 350°F. Spray two baking sheets with cooking spray.
2. In a large bowl, combine flours, sugar, salt, and baking powder.
3. In a medium bowl, combine oil, egg, milk, and vanilla. Add to the dry ingredients and mix thoroughly to form a dough.
4. Drop cookie dough balls about 2" apart on baking sheet.
5. Bake 8–10 minutes or until slightly browned on edges. Let cool slightly before serving.

PECAN CAKE

Classy Capricorns crave a dessert as elegant as they are—so please, leave frosting and sprinkles out of the equation! Down-to-earth Capricorns prefer desserts featuring whole foods and natural sweeteners, which is why you'll be star struck by this buttery Pecan Cake! Lightly glazed with an orange marmalade reduction, practical sea goats will appreciate the delicate sweetness of this simple and classy cake. No, you don't have the most demanding sweet tooth, dear Capricorn, but when the occasion arises, your expert baking skills always turn out a stellar dessert! No doubt, you'll shine once more when you serve up this delicious Pecan Cake!

SERVES 6

3 large eggs, divided
1 cup pecans, divided
½ cup butter
¾ cup cake flour
1 teaspoon baking powder

⅔ cup plus ¼ cup granulated sugar, divided
1 tablespoon lemon juice
½ teaspoon salt
½ cup orange marmalade

1. Preheat oven to 350°F. Grease and flour a 9" round cake pan.
2. Separate eggs. Finely grate ½ cup pecans. Melt butter in a small saucepan over low heat.
3. In a medium bowl, blend together flour and baking powder.
4. In a large mixing bowl, beat egg yolks until they are thick and lemon-colored. Gradually beat in 2/3 cup sugar. Beat in lemon juice and grated pecans. Gradually beat in the flour mixture. Slowly beat in melted butter.
5. In a small bowl, beat egg whites with salt until stiff peaks form. Fold the beaten egg whites into the batter.
6. Pour the batter into prepared pan.
7. Bake 30–35 minutes or until a toothpick inserted in the center comes out clean. Let the cake cool 10 minutes before removing from the pan.
8. In a small saucepan over medium-low heat, combine orange marmalade and remaining ¼ cup sugar. Cook until sugar is dissolved, stirring constantly. While still warm, pour this glaze over the cake. Garnish cake with remaining whole pecans.

NEGRONI

Ambitious Capricorns prefer a straight-up classy drink. No to frills, yes to bitters. Look no further than the Negroni. This substantial Italian cocktail features Campari, a bitters liqeur, which lends the Negroni its signature red hue and its emblematic bitter profile that Capricorn sea goats crave. Equal parts make this recipe easy to remember by heart, and even easier to make. This is one prestigious concoction that's sure to impress both you and your guests!

SERVES 1

1 ounce gin
1 ounce sweet vermouth

1 ounce Campari
1 orange twist

1. Pour the liquid ingredients into a shaker. Shake and strain into a rocks glass of ice.
2. Garnish with orange twist.

Aquarius:
The Scientist Chef

Aquarians are intelligent and freethinking air signs with egalitarian ideals. Their progressive ideas often seem ahead of the curve, and yet, they are as scientific and logical as they come. Highly individualistic, Aquarians thrive in group settings as individuals who are both part of the group and yet coolly unique. These gregarious air signs understand the value of networking. Leave it to Aquarius to "know a guy who knows a guy." Masters of casualness, Aquarians are represented as the water bearer—a human being holding a vase of fresh water—a symbol of human innovation and progress.

Aquarians are the coolest nerds around. These low-key eccentrics are fascinated with technology—a symbol of progress in and of itself. The Aquarian kitchen is geeked out with gadgets, complete with an air fryer, an ergonomic pineapple corer, and a sous vide. They are always surprising guests with quirky kitchen hacks as they elevate their dishes with their eclectic culinary gear. Social Aquarians believe mealtime is an opportunity to connect, so you can look forward to wowing your guests at your next party with Tofu Thai Kebabs or Barbecued Pork Ribs. These friendly air signs love planning luncheons under the guise of business; however, they really just want to catch up!

SKILLET FRITTATA

Ingenious Aquarians love any excuse they get to use a cast-iron skillet, so here's your shining moment, water bearer! If it's been forever since you've used your beloved cast-iron, you'll want to re-season before use. Fresh herbs elevate eggs to the next level of delicious in this dish while also contributing to the frittata's gorgeous bursts of green. We won't put it past you to alter the vegetable lineup, opinionated Aquarius; just don't forget the feta cheese! Feta brings an irresistible tanginess to this dish that unites all the frittata's flavors into cohesiveness. Harmony is satisfying to you, Aquarius, and so is this delicious Skillet Frittata!

SERVES 6

1 tablespoon unsalted butter
1 tablespoon olive oil
1 small onion, peeled and diced
1 pound asparagus, chopped and bottoms trimmed
¼ cup fresh or frozen peas
1 cup crumbled feta cheese
1 tablespoon minced fresh oregano

1 tablespoon minced fresh dill
1 tablespoon minced fresh Italian parsley
½ tablespoon minced fresh basil
½ teaspoon sea salt
½ teaspoon ground black pepper
7 large eggs

1. Preheat oven to 325°F.
2. Heat butter and oil in a 12" cast-iron skillet over medium heat. Add onion, asparagus, and peas and sauté until onions are soft.
3. Meanwhile, in a medium bowl, whisk together feta, oregano, dill, parsley, basil, salt, pepper, and eggs.
4. Pour the egg mixture over the vegetables in the skillet. Tilt the skillet slightly to coat all of the ingredients with the egg mixture. Cook over medium heat until the eggs are just beginning to set, about 8–12 minutes.
5. Place in oven and bake 10 minutes or until the mixture is cooked through and just beginning to brown.
6. Remove from the pan and slice. Serve immediately.

AVOCADO BAGEL SANDWICH

According to you, opinionated Aquarius, bagels are the best breakfast. Objectively speaking, of course! Handheld, open to interpretation, and easy to eat on the move—hey, no one can argue with that, Aquarius! So here's a solid bagel sandwich that you can add to your breakfast repertoire! Alfalfa sprouts, avocado, and cream cheese seem to be a perfect pairing for you, astute Aquarius. But for those mornings when you have a little more time to spare, you'll have all the reason you need to add crispy bacon to this handheld nosh. Now that's ideal!

SERVES 1

2 ounces whipped cream cheese
1 whole-wheat bagel, sliced
1 slice tomato
1 slice peeled red onion

½ medium avocado, peeled, pitted, and sliced
¼ cup alfalfa sprouts

1. Spread cream cheese on both halves of bagel.
2. Layer tomato, onion, avocado, and alfalfa sprouts on the bottom half of the bagel.
3. Top with the other half of bagel and cut the sandwich in half. Serve.

BLUEBERRY BANANA SMOOTHIE

Ruled by practical Saturn, you know that the best things in life are not overly complicated. A banana and blueberry smoothie? Perfect combo. You've had plenty of these smoothies in life. What's not to love? But then again, the inventive Aquarian mind is always looking for ways to evolve and advance what's tried-and-true. Here's just the ticket for you, revolutionary Aquarius. This smoothie takes on a low-key tropical vibe with the addition of coconut milk, lime, and honey. Futuristic Aquarians can enjoy this ultra-refreshing smoothie after a workout or to stay cool during the workday.

YIELDS 1½ CUPS

1 medium banana, peeled
1 cup blueberries
½ cup coconut milk

2 tablespoons raw honey
Juice of 1 small lime
1 cup ice

1. Combine all the ingredients in a blender and purée until smooth.
2. Serve immediately.

∘∘∘∘ CHILL OUT ∘∘∘∘

As the electric air sign of the zodiac, your mind moves more rapidly than most. This is an amazing quality for great thinkers like you; however, it can also be stressful on your nervous system. Blueberries and coconut milk are excellent nerve-toning tonics. So you can rest assured: This icy beverage will chill you out in more ways than one!

PAD THAI

Research proves that Aquarians love Pad Thai, statistically speaking, of course. Characterized by slightly spicy noodles, a dash of scrambled eggs, and crushed peanuts for an irresistible crunch, Pad Thai is a distinctively flavorful and supremely satisfying dish that objective Aquarians routinely enjoy. Here's an easy recipe that will help inventive Aquarians graduate from take-out (we know you'll be up to the challenge). Surprisingly simple to make, this version features shrimp, but feel free to elect another protein like cubed tofu or chicken. Just don't forget the sriracha, quixotic Aquarius!

SERVES 4

¼ pound dried rice noodles

3 tablespoons rice vinegar

1 tablespoon fish sauce

2 tablespoons granulated sugar

1 teaspoon Chinese chili paste with garlic

1 tablespoon peanut oil

3 cloves garlic, minced

1 large egg, beaten

½ pound medium shrimp, peeled and deveined

2 cups mung bean sprouts

½ cup sliced green onions

¼ cup chopped peanuts

---

1. Place noodles in a large bowl and cover with warm water. Let soak until noodles are soft, about 20 minutes. Drain noodles well and set aside.
2. In a small bowl, combine rice vinegar, fish sauce, sugar, and chili paste and mix well; set aside.
3. Have all the remaining ingredients ready. In a wok or large skillet, heat peanut oil over medium-high heat. Add garlic; cook until golden, about 15 seconds. Add egg; stir-fry until set, about 30 seconds. Add shrimp and stir-fry until pink, about 2 minutes.
4. Add noodles, tossing with tongs until they soften and curl, about 1 minute. Add bean sprouts and green onions; stir-fry for 1 minute.
5. Stir the vinegar mixture and add to wok; stir-fry until the mixture is hot, about 1–2 minutes longer. Sprinkle with peanuts and serve immediately.

SWEET AND SPICY ALMONDS

These logical air signs are always snacking on the go. So here's an easy-to-transport and intrinsically energizing snack that all breezy Aquarians will enjoy: almonds! Methodical Aquarians are always down to reinvent something they already know and love, so this recipe gives you the know-how to produce your own DIY flavored almonds. You'll adore the spicy sweetness of this healthy snack, but take warning: This is one addictive snack you may not be able to put down!

SERVES 8

1 tablespoon olive oil
2 cups whole almonds
1 tablespoon granulated sugar

1 teaspoon cayenne pepper
1 teaspoon chipotle powder
½ teaspoon chili powder

1. Preheat oven to 250°F. Line two baking sheets with parchment paper.
2. In a medium bowl, toss all the ingredients together. Make sure the nuts are evenly coated.
3. Arrange almonds in a single layer on one of the baking sheets and bake 25 minutes or until the almonds look mostly dry, stirring every 5 minutes.
4. Remove from oven. Pour onto the remaining lined baking sheet to cool.

JALAPEÑO CORN BREAD

Aquarians are natural networkers who thrive in group settings. Gregarious Aquarians know how to keep conversation cool, light, and interesting—winning us over with their ability to be both unique and relatable. So here's a dish that everyone loves and yet has its own eccentric flair: Jalapeño Corn Bread! Jalapeño gives beloved corn bread a distinctive and refreshing zing that cool Aquarius can appreciate. You'll know your corn bread is baked to perfection when a toothpick inserted in the center comes out clean. Pair this dish with the Skillet Frittata or the Barbecued Pork Ribs (see recipes in this chapter) and a slather of butter for an extrastellar meal.

SERVES 4

- 1 small yellow onion, peeled and chopped into ¼" pieces
- 2 cloves garlic, minced
- 2 tablespoons canned chopped jalapeños, drained
- 1½ cups bread flour
- ¾ cup masa harina or cornmeal
- ¼ cup granulated sugar
- 4½ teaspoons baking powder
- 1 teaspoon salt
- 1 large egg
- 1 cup whole milk
- ½ teaspoon vegetable oil
- ½ cup canned cream-style corn
- ½ cup grated Cheddar cheese

1. Preheat oven to 350°F.
2. In a medium mixing bowl, combine all the ingredients together.
3. Pour the mixture into a greased bread pan. Bake 30–45 minutes or until lightly brown on top. Serve warm or at room temperature.

CLASSIC CHICKEN PARMESAN

Humanitarian Aquarians believe that whoever invented breaded chicken deserves an award. These socially conscious air signs will always adore a classic yet clever dish like Classic Chicken Parmesan. Air signs always need a filling and incredibly delicious dish like this one. Breaded chicken baked with marinara sauce, dried herbs, and a generous layer of cheese—this is the perfect lunch for Aquarians to enjoy midday. Freethinking Aquarians can decide between enjoying their chicken cutlets on their own, on spaghetti, or even in a sub sandwich.

SERVES 10

3½ pounds boneless, skinless chicken breasts

3 large eggs

1 cup plain bread crumbs

¾ cup all-purpose flour

2 tablespoons olive oil

2 cups marinara sauce, divided

2 teaspoons dried basil

2 teaspoons dried oregano

1 teaspoon ground black pepper

1 pound mozzarella or provolone cheese, shredded

¼ cup sliced scallions (ends trimmed), for garnish

---

1. Preheat oven to 375°F. Rinse the chicken in ice-cold water and pat dry with paper towels.
2. Beat eggs in a shallow bowl. Place bread crumbs in a separate shallow bowl. Place flour in a third shallow bowl. Lightly dust chicken with flour, then dip it in egg, and lastly coat it in bread crumbs.
3. Heat oil over medium-high heat in a large sauté pan. Add the breaded chicken and quickly brown on each side, remove, and drain on paper towels.
4. Ladle ½ cup marinara in the bottom of a baking pan. Place the chicken in the pan in a single layer. Top with remaining sauce and season with basil, oregano, and pepper. Top with cheese.
5. Bake 20 minutes. Garnish with chopped scallions and serve.

ROASTED GARLIC MASHED POTATOES

Quick-witted Aquarians may be inventive, but they are also practical. That's why you're whipping up everyone's favorite buttery, fluffy side: mashed potatoes! The kicker, you ask? Three heads of garlic! Aquarians are well aware of garlic's potent health benefits, but they also know that garlic intrinsically belongs in mashed potatoes—abundantly. Friendly water bearers need not worry—the pungency of the garlic mellows down as it cooks, so you can confidently go about your social activities after you eat without worrying about how much garlic you ate.

SERVES 6
---

3 heads garlic
2 pounds red bliss potatoes, peeled and
   cut into large chunks
8 tablespoons butter

½ cup milk or cream
1½ teaspoons salt
⅛ teaspoon ground white pepper

---

1. Preheat oven to 350°F. Wrap all three garlic heads in a pouch fashioned from aluminum foil and place in the center of oven. Roast until garlic is very soft and yields to gentle finger pressure, about 1 hour and 15 minutes. Allow garlic to cool to the touch and then cut garlic bulbs in half laterally. Using your hands, squeeze out the roasted garlic and push it through a sieve.
2. In a large pot with enough lightly salted water to cover potatoes, boil potatoes until very tender, about 25–30 minutes depending on size of potato pieces. Drain potatoes well, then return them to the pot. Place pot on the stove and cook over medium heat for 30 seconds to 1 minute to steam off any excess moisture.
3. In a small saucepan over medium-low heat, heat butter and milk together until butter melts.
4. For smoothest mashed potatoes, force potatoes through a ricer. Otherwise, mash them with a potato masher or stiff wire whisk.
5. Add roasted garlic purée, salt, pepper, and the butter mixture to the potatoes and mix just enough to incorporate. Serve immediately.

PASTA E FAGIOLI
(Pasta and Bean Soup)

*Noble Aquarians will salivate over this hearty tomato-based soup.
A popular favorite with infinite variations, "pasta e fagioli" simply translates
to "pasta and beans." This recipe gives you chickpeas, aromatic parsley, and
some vegetables, but the pasta is up to you, inventive Aquarius!
Ditalini is most commonly used, though we wouldn't put it past you
to use gluten-free dinosaur-shaped pasta. Either way,
water bearer, this soup is sure to satisfy!*

SERVES 10

1 pound dried chickpeas

4 gallons vegetable stock, divided

2 tablespoons olive oil

4 medium shallots, peeled and finely chopped

1 bulb garlic, finely chopped

2 medium celery roots, finely chopped

2 pounds plum tomatoes, cored and chopped

½ bunch fresh parsley, chopped

2 cups cooked bite-sized pasta of choice

½ cup fresh-grated Asiago cheese

1 teaspoon ground black pepper

1. Sort through chickpeas, discarding any stones. In a large stockpot over medium heat, simmer chickpeas in 2 gallons stock for approximately 2–3 hours until tender. Drain and set chickpeas aside.

2. In same stockpot over medium heat, heat oil. Sauté shallots, garlic, and celeriac 3 minutes. Add tomatoes and sauté 1 minute. Add remaining stock, chickpeas, and parsley. Let simmer 1 hour uncovered.

3. Just before serving, stir in pasta. Sprinkle each serving with cheese and pepper.

CREAMY CAESAR SALAD

Fortunately and unfortunately for you, political Aquarius, the Caesar Salad was not named for Julius Caesar, but for Caesar Cardini, who created this iconic salad in Tijuana, Mexico, during the Prohibition era. Inventive Aquarians are easily captivated by this salad's refreshing romaine crunch and the alluringly unique anchovy dressing. But wait, it gets better: This recipe gives you everything you need to make your own creamy, lemony, cheesy dressing. It doesn't get any fresher than this, idealistic Aquarius! Leftover dressing can be stored in the refrigerator up to 1 week—but we see an abundance of Creamy Caesar Salads in your future, so it'll go quick!

SERVES 6

- 2 cloves garlic, chopped
- 3 large egg yolks
- 1 tablespoon Dijon mustard
- 3 tablespoons Worcestershire sauce
- 1 tablespoon anchovy paste or 2 anchovy fillets
- ½ cup grated Parmesan cheese, divided
- 2 tablespoons fresh lemon juice, divided

- ½ teaspoon salt
- 1 teaspoon ground black pepper
- 1 tablespoon water
- 1 cup light olive oil
- 1 head romaine lettuce, chopped
- ½ cup chopped cooked bacon
- 1 cup croutons

1. In a food processor, place garlic, egg yolks, mustard, Worcestershire sauce, anchovy paste, ¼ cup Parmesan cheese, 1 tablespoon lemon juice, salt, pepper, and water. Process until dressing is combined and thick. With the processor running, slowly add oil until well incorporated.
2. In a large bowl, combine lettuce and remaining lemon juice. Add just enough dressing to coat lettuce (add more if you want to make it creamier). Toss in bacon and croutons. Top salad with remaining Parmesan. Serve with extra dressing.

LINGUINE WITH ASPARAGUS, PARMESAN, AND CREAM

*Humanitarian Aquarians will adore this creamy pasta dish bolstered with
the bright acidic notes of white wine and fresh lemon. Sautéed shallots add
another valuable dimension to this dish, and asparagus also chimes in.
Pasta is as dependable as it comes for realistic Aquarians, and yet, this dish
possesses a unique flair that eccentric Aquarians will appreciate.
This is one dish that outspoken Aquarians will want to savor,
take big bites of, and appreciate.*

SERVES 6

- 1 bunch asparagus (preferably chubby-stemmed), bottoms trimmed
- 2 teaspoons olive oil
- 2 medium shallots, peeled and thinly sliced
- ¼ cup white wine
- ¼ cup vegetable stock
- 2 cups heavy cream
- 8 ounces linguine, cooked al dente, drained, and tossed with a drop of olive oil
- ¼ cup Parmigiano-Reggiano cheese
- Juice of 1 medium lemon, plus 6 lemon wedges
- ⅛ teaspoon kosher salt
- ⅛ teaspoon ground black pepper

1. Use a vegetable peeler to peel off the skin from the bottom half of asparagus stalks. Cut asparagus into bite-sized (about 1") pieces.
2. In a large skillet over medium heat, warm oil. Add shallots and cook 3 minutes to soften them.
3. Add asparagus and wine; cook until wine is mostly evaporated, then add stock.
4. When asparagus are mostly cooked and stock is mostly steamed out, stir in cream and bring to a boil.
5. Add linguine. Cook until linguine is hot and the sauce is slightly thick. Add cheese and remove from heat.
6. Season with lemon juice, salt, and pepper. Serve with lemon wedges on the side.

BEEF AND POLENTA CASSEROLE

Edgy Aquarians will undoubtedly be intrigued by this lasagna-inspired polenta casserole. And yes, this dish is outstandingly delicious! Polenta is a highly versatile cornmeal mixture that inventive Aquarians can't resist. Sure, you have worked with store-bought polenta, but this time, it's homemade so that you can more easily spread it into your casserole dish. Egalitarian Aquarians will appreciate that this can also be converted to a vegetarian dish by swapping out ground beef in favor of black beans and more vegetables.

SERVES 10

POLENTA

5 cups water
¼ cup unsalted butter
1¼ cups cornmeal

CASSEROLE

2 tablespoons olive oil, divided
2 medium Vidalia onions, peeled and diced
1 medium shallot, peeled and minced

1 bulb garlic, minced
1½ pounds lean ground beef
4 medium tomatoes, cored and sliced
1 bunch steamed escarole (or any bitter greens)
½ cup ricotta
3 sprigs basil, chopped
½ teaspoon ground black pepper
½ cup freshly grated Romano cheese
2 tablespoons melted unsalted butter

1. In a large saucepan, heat water and butter to a simmer over medium to medium-high heat. Slowly whisk in cornmeal, stirring constantly to avoid lumps.
2. Reduce heat to low. Cook 20–25 minutes uncovered, stirring frequently until thick and creamy. Set aside.
3. Preheat oven to 350°F. Grease a large casserole dish with 1 tablespoon oil.
4. Heat remaining oil over medium heat in a large skillet. Add onions, shallot, garlic, and beef. Sauté 10–15 minutes until beef is browned. Drain off excess grease.
5. Spread a thin layer of polenta in the bottom of prepared casserole dish. Spread layers of beef, tomatoes, escarole, ricotta, basil, and pepper on top. Top with remaining polenta. Sprinkle with Romano cheese. Drizzle with butter.
6. Bake 20 minutes and serve.

BARBECUED PORK RIBS

Aquarians are quick-moving, but they also understand patience and strategy, which makes them masters of barbecue—just ask fellow Aquarian and celebrity chef Guy Fieri! Techy Aquarians can achieve the tenderest of ribs with their smoker, while minimalistic Aquarians can masterfully work the grill (or hey, even the oven works too). With so many variables in preparing the perfect rack of ribs, cook time will depend on your keen observations, scientific Aquarius. You'll know when the ribs are done when you bend them into a "U" shape and the meat breaks open in the middle.

SERVES 4

8 fresh chipotle chilies, stems removed
½ cup water
1 small red onion, peeled and cut into ¼" pieces
12 garlic cloves, minced
¼ cup red wine vinegar

1 cup honey
½ cup Dijon mustard
1 tablespoon dried oregano
1 teaspoon salt
1 teaspoon ground black pepper
4 pounds pork ribs

1. Preheat grill to medium setting.
2. Place chilies in a small saucepan with the water; cover and simmer on low setting 10 minutes or until chilies are plump. Drain off water. Cut chilies into ¼" pieces.
3. Combine all the remaining ingredients except ribs in a medium saucepan; stir well. Bring the mixture to a boil. Cover and simmer 10 minutes. Reserve ½ cup to be used as a dipping sauce with the meal.
4. Use remainder of sauce to baste ribs while grilling. Grill ribs about 2–3 hours, then serve.

∘ ∘ ∘ ∘ **THROW A BARBECUE PARTY!** ∘ ∘ ∘ ∘

Cool Aquarians don't get emotional very often, but this smoky, sweet barbecue sauce is sure to excite! If you need to feed a lot of hungry people, double (or triple) this recipe and invite your friends and family to share—and of course, to hang out with you while you work the grill, social Aquarius!

THAI TOFU KEBABS

Since Aquarians are so humbly humanitarian, you'll also serve these astronomical vegan kebabs at your weekend barbecue! These kebabs are exploding with flavor and are guaranteed to be a hot item (literally) at your party! Just one word of caution to even the most rebellious water bearers: Bird's Eye peppers are ferociously hot. This tiny Thai capsaicin proves that a little goes a long way—blending exquisitely with lime, Thai basil, and cooling lemongrass. Just be mindful handling the Bird's Eyes and wash your hands immediately afterward. We can always count on you, worldly Aquarius, to throw a party with provoking banter and out-of-this-world food that everyone loves.

SERVES 4

2 pounds extra-firm tofu
6 medium Thai eggplants, halved
2 medium red onions, peeled and cut
  into wedges
½ cup chopped Thai basil
¼ cup olive oil
⅓ cup lime juice

¼ cup thick Thai soy sauce
2 tablespoons minced lemongrass
2 tablespoons minced galangal
2 tablespoons minced ginger
2 tablespoons palm sugar
2 Thai Bird's Eye peppers, minced

1. Place all the ingredients in a resealable plastic bag. Shake to evenly distribute. Refrigerate 4 hours.
2. Once marinated, thread tofu, eggplant, and onion wedges alternately on 8–10 bamboo skewers.
3. Place the skewers on a nonstick grill pan and grill on each side until tofu is golden, about 5–10 minutes. Serve.

CARAMEL SOUR CREAM CAKE

When it comes to dessert, these gregarious air signs reach for the fluffiest cakes they can find. Caramel is one thing cool Aquarians unabashedly lust after. The water bearer can count their lucky stars because this cake boasts a double dose of those lovable notes of caramel—both within its exemplary cake batter, as well as in its delectable caramel frosting. You'll play it casual, Aquarius, but we know you won't be able to resist this stellar dessert!

SERVES 16

CAKE

1 cup sour cream
½ cup granulated sugar
½ cup brown sugar
2 large eggs
2 teaspoons vanilla extract
1¾ cups all-purpose flour
1 teaspoon baking powder
1 teaspoon baking soda
¼ teaspoon salt
¼ teaspoon ground nutmeg

CARAMEL FROSTING

1 (14-ounce) can condensed milk
1 cup brown sugar
2 tablespoons butter
1 teaspoon vanilla extract

1. Preheat oven to 350°F. Grease a 9" × 13" pan with unsalted butter and set aside.
2. In a large bowl, combine sour cream and granulated sugar and beat well. Add brown sugar and beat. Add eggs, one at a time, beating well after each addition. Stir in vanilla.
3. In a medium bowl, sift flour with baking powder, baking soda, salt, and nutmeg. Stir into the sour cream mixture and beat at medium speed for 1 minute. Pour into prepared pan.
4. Bake 25–35 minutes or until cake pulls away from sides of pan and top springs back when lightly touched in center. Cool completely on a wire rack.
5. Place the frosting ingredients in a small saucepan and bring to a boil. Then turn down heat and simmer 8 minutes. Remove from heat and let frosting cool and condense 5 minutes. Apply to cake once both are cooled down.

PEANUT BUTTER CHOCOLATE BARS

Quirky Aquarians can nerd out over these chocolaty Peanut Butter Chocolate Bars. Baked with oatmeal and crushed peanut butter cereal, this dessert carries the perfect amount of crunch and saltiness that air signs like you crave in a dessert. These scrumptious peanut butter squares are the perfect sweet midday indulgence to help you survive the rest of your day. Or enjoy them as an after-dinner dessert paired with a scoop of your favorite ice cream. Don't try to figure out what makes these bars so delicious, scientific Aquarius; just eat and enjoy!

YIELDS 36 BARS

5 tablespoons butter, softened
⅓ cup peanut butter
1 large egg
1 large egg white
1 cup brown sugar
1 cup all-purpose flour
¾ cup crisp peanut butter–flavored cereal squares, finely crushed

1 cup quick-cooking oatmeal
¼ teaspoon salt
½ teaspoon baking soda
1 (13-ounce) can nonfat sweetened condensed milk
2 cups semisweet chocolate chips, divided

1. Preheat oven to 350°F. Spray a 9" × 13" baking pan with nonstick cooking spray containing flour; set aside.
2. In a large bowl, combine butter, peanut butter, egg, and egg white and beat until combined. Add brown sugar and beat until smooth.
3. Stir in flour, cereal, oatmeal, salt, and baking soda and mix until crumbly. Press half into prepared pan.
4. In a medium microwave-safe bowl, combine sweetened condensed milk and 1½ cups chocolate chips; microwave on 50 percent power for 2 minutes, then remove and stir until smooth. Spoon evenly over the crumbs in pan.
5. Top with remaining ½ cup chocolate chips, then remaining crumbs; press down lightly.
6. Bake 20–25 minutes or until bars are set. Cool completely, then cut into squares to serve.

MANHATTAN

*Aquarians will never turn down a Manhattan—the quintessential cocktail
of old-timey cool meets modern-day hipster. Intellectual Aquarians are
all about rye whiskey, which means that you'll adore this particularly
substantial cocktail featuring mostly whiskey (and a cherry on top). This
drink is named for a certain trendsetting apex of the world. Aquarians
appreciate feeling plugged in, and one way you can do that, dear
Aquarius, is by gathering friends and sipping on Manhattans
as you divulge your plans for world takeover.*

SERVES 1

2 ounces rye whiskey

½ ounce sweet vermouth

2 dashes Angostura bitters

1 cherry

Pour the liquid ingredients into a shaker. Shake and strain into a cocktail glass. Garnish
with cherry. Manhattans can also be served on the rocks.

Pisces:
The Intuitive Chef

Mystical Pisces are represented by two celestial fish. Pisceans are truly enigmatic, compassionate souls with vivid imaginations and a fantastically unique sense of humor. Pisceans live in their own private world as the undercover star of their own life movie. Fluent in nonverbal communication, these intuitive water signs soulfully connect with the messages emoted through music, art, poetry, and film. Mutable Pisces can adapt to any environment, though they are also psychic sponges who need to regularly retreat from the world. Every celestial fish has at least one ritualistic escape hatch they can swim to—be it popcorn and a movie, their yoga mat, or the local dive bar.

Pisceans seek magic, and one place they find it is in the kitchen! Whimsical Pisceans cook intuitively, allowing their senses to guide them. In fact, these celestial sea creatures often forgo measurements altogether, adding spices until their ancestors tell them to stop. Leave it to Pisces to put their fantastical creative flair on every dish (which often features a rare ingredient)—whether it's their creative finesse of their Jelly Roll or the extraordinary plating of their Pecan Fish with Sweet Potatoes. With a carefulness to set the mood, mealtime is always a ritual for these creative visionaries, so if this ethereal starlet invites you to their table, it's sure to be memorable!

CHILI MASALA TOFU SCRAMBLE

Pisces are chameleonlike sea creatures who take on the qualities of their surroundings. Similarly, tofu does the exact same thing! And maybe this is just one reason why intuitive Pisceans adore a delicious Chili Masala Tofu Scramble. Turmeric gives the tofu a yellow color, evocative of scrambled eggs, while a medley of vegetables and spices offers you the energizing kick you crave to get you moving in the morning. This breakfast gives you all the reason you need to fly out of bed and seize the day.

SERVES 2

- 1 (14-ounce) container firm or extra-firm tofu, pressed
- 1 small onion, peeled and diced
- 2 cloves garlic, minced
- 2 tablespoons olive oil
- 1 small red chili pepper, minced
- 1 medium green bell pepper, seeded and chopped
- ¾ cup sliced mushrooms
- 1 tablespoon soy sauce
- 1 teaspoon curry powder
- ½ teaspoon ground cumin
- ¼ teaspoon turmeric
- 1 teaspoon nutritional yeast (optional)

1. Cut or crumble pressed tofu into 1" cubes.
2. In a medium skillet over medium-high heat, sauté onion and garlic in olive oil 1–2 minutes until onions are soft.
3. Add tofu, chili pepper, bell pepper, and mushrooms, stirring well to combine.
4. Add the remaining ingredients, except nutritional yeast, and combine well. Allow to cook until tofu is lightly browned, about 6–8 minutes.
5. Remove from heat and stir in nutritional yeast if desired. Serve.

○ ○ ○ ○ **TOFU PREP** ○ ○ ○ ○

Tofu is packaged in water, which isn't the most compatible with hot oil. Optimize your morning (and your tofu) by draining, slicing, and pressing your tofu the night before. Refrigerate the pressed tofu in an airtight container, and you'll be ready to rock and roll in the morning.

BREAKFAST BAKLAVA FRENCH TOAST

*You might be a water sign, Pisces, but your head is often in the clouds.
For breakfast, you'll transfer yourself straight to cloud nine with this
transcendently delicious Breakfast Baklava French Toast. Dreamy Pisceans
will blissfully anticipate the sweet, nutty baklava filling layered between two
slices of French toast. Mystical Pisces can level up their breakfast game with
thick, fluffy cuts of brioche or challah, and by topping with whipped cream.
Now you're truly living the dream, Pisces!*

SERVES 2

3 large eggs
2 tablespoons orange juice
1 teaspoon grated orange zest
⅛ teaspoon vanilla extract
¼ cup plus 1 tablespoon honey, divided
2 tablespoons whole milk
¾ teaspoon ground cinnamon, divided
¼ cup chopped walnuts

¼ cup chopped blanched almonds
¼ teaspoon ground cloves
1 tablespoon granulated sugar
2 tablespoons white bread crumbs or
   ground melba toast
4 slices bread
2 tablespoons unsalted butter
1 teaspoon confectioners' sugar

---

1. In a large bowl, whisk together eggs, orange juice, zest, vanilla, ¼ cup honey, milk, and ¼ teaspoon cinnamon. Set aside.
2. In a food processor, pulse walnuts and almonds until they are finely crumbled. Transfer nuts to a small bowl and add cloves, ¼ teaspoon cinnamon, sugar, and bread crumbs. Stir to combine.
3. Sandwich half the walnut and almond mixture between two slices bread. Repeat with remaining two slices. Carefully dunk both sides of the sandwiches into the egg mixture. Make sure the egg mixture soaks into the bread.
4. Add butter to a large skillet over medium heat and heat 30 seconds. Add sandwiches and fry 2 minutes per side or until golden.
5. Place each sandwich on a plate and cut them vertically. Dust with confectioners' sugar. Top with remaining honey and sprinkle with ¼ teaspoon cinnamon. Serve immediately.

GINGER PEACHY SMOOTHIE

Dreamy Pisces, when you're looking for an excuse to drift away from your desk midday, all the reason you need is this Ginger Peachy Smoothie! This divinely delicious concoction is sure to transport the celestial fish's senses. Sweet peaches are even sweeter when they are fresh, but if peaches are not in season, frozen peaches will work great—just add water instead of ice. Ginger naturally energizes, helping Pisces to stay focused during the afternoon lull, while high-protein yogurt keeps you level. Delicious and interesting, this smoothie is certain to capture your heart, Pisces.

YIELDS 1½ CUPS

3 large yellow or white peaches, pitted
1 (¼") piece ginger

1 cup low-fat vanilla yogurt
½ cup ice

1. Combine all the ingredients in a blender and purée until smooth.
2. Serve immediately.

◦ ◦ ◦ ◦ **JUST PEACHY** ◦ ◦ ◦ ◦

With vibrant imaginations and vivid dreams (both waking and asleep), imaginative Pisces are ruled by Jupiter—planet of faith, abundance, and travel. Jupiter represents the juiciness that life has to offer, so it's no wonder that Jupiter also rules peaches!

SMOKED SALMON AND MASCARPONE-STUFFED PITA POCKETS

If you love a lox bagel, then you'll love this unique and tasty take on lunch, visionary Pisces. Smoked salmon and mascarpone are a heavenly match made for enigmatic Pisceans to devour. Green peppercorns add ideal notes of acidity and spice to elevate this melted cheese pita sandwich to the divinely delicious heights you dream of. If you can't find peppercorns, capers work great as well! You like to go with the flow, Pisces, but this is one lunch you'll eagerly swim toward.

SERVES 2

2 whole-wheat pita pockets
2 thin slices peeled red onion
2 thin slices peeled lemon, seeded
⅛ pound smoked salmon

⅛ pound mascarpone cheese, sliced
1 teaspoon green peppercorns, packed in brine
⅛ teaspoon ground black pepper

1. Preheat oven to 350°F.
2. Using half of ingredients for each pocket, stuff the pockets with onion, lemon, salmon, cheese, peppercorns, and black pepper.
3. Bake 15–20 minutes until pitas are golden and the filling is hot. Serve.

BUDDHA BOWL

Pisceans tend to be spiritually inclined—from their crystal collection and religious iconography to their candles and seashells, Pisces love a good ritual! But right now, your favorite ritual is lunch. No matter your practice, dear Pisces, you'll love this Buddha Bowl! A classic vegan rice bowl, this colorful dish is loaded with vegetables, protein, and bold flavor to elevate your spirits and satisfy your belly midday. There's plenty of room for creative Pisces to play with flavors in this dish. Brown rice could be cooked with garlic or tossed with toasted sesame oil. Let your whimsical tastes lead, dreamy Pisces!

SERVES 4

1 cup broccoli florets
1 small red onion, peeled and chopped
1 medium carrot, peeled and grated
1 medium avocado, peeled, pitted, and diced
¼ cup sliced kalamata olives
3 ounces extra-firm tofu, cubed

1 medium beet, cooked and cubed
1 cup cooked chickpeas
2 tablespoons rice vinegar
1 teaspoon ground black pepper
1 tablespoon avocado oil
2 cups hot or cold cooked brown rice

Place all the ingredients in a large bowl and toss to combine, then serve.

PREMIERE POPCORN

For those low-key evenings when you're settling into your chill home vibes, you crave a spectacular snack for when the movie starts. This popcorn isn't just any movie popcorn; it's popcorn with bacon! That's right—crispy, salty, sweet, and divinely decadent bacon. As if freshly sizzled bacon weren't enough to make your popcorn dreams come true, crunchy french-fried onions are also added to the mix. Pop kernels over the stove, or, if you're unsure, microwave popcorn is fine, but aim for the plainest flavor, as you'll be adding your own spicy buttery topping. This is one snack worth dreaming about, Pisces!

SERVES 8

1 pound bacon
½ cup butter
1 teaspoon chili powder
¼ teaspoon garlic salt

¼ teaspoon onion salt
½ teaspoon paprika
4 quarts popped popcorn
1 cup canned french-fried onions

1. Preheat oven to 250°F.
2. Cook bacon in a large frying pan until very crisp. Drain off the grease and transfer bacon to paper towels to cool. When cool, crumble bacon into small pieces.
3. In a small saucepan over low heat, melt butter. Add chili powder, garlic salt, onion salt, and paprika; stir until well blended.
4. Pour the butter mixture over popcorn and toss until well covered.
5. Add bacon and canned onions to popcorn and toss lightly.
6. Pour the mixture onto a baking sheet. Bake 10 minutes. Serve.

SEVEN-INGREDIENT ANCHOVY FUSILLI

Flowing Pisces will be intrigued by the cook method of this dish. Usually pasta is boiled in water, but this time, our pasta spirals are slow-cooked in chicken stock, allowing them to absorb more flavor. This showstopping pasta will positively make Pisces swoon. Poetic Pisces might like to riff on this recipe by adding sun-dried tomatoes to the mix or a light sprinkle of Parmesan cheese. Enjoy as an appetizer or as its own meal.
Buon appetito!

SERVES 8

16 ounces fusilli

4 (15-ounce) cans low-sodium chicken broth

2 (10-ounce) cans anchovies packed in oil, chopped

¼ cup olive oil

1 clove garlic, finely chopped

¼ cup chopped fresh parsley

1 teaspoon salt

1. Place pasta and chicken broth in a 6-quart slow cooker. Cook on high 30 minutes, check for doneness, and cook an additional 15 minutes if needed.
2. Stir in anchovies, olive oil, and garlic. Sprinkle with parsley and salt. Remove from heat and serve.

∘∘∘∘ PISCES GLAMOUR ∘∘∘∘

Enigmatic Pisceans' heightened compassion often leads them into helping and healing professions, but also into the arts! Sensitive Pisces are gifted poets, melody masters, and painters. Their innate chameleonlike nature allows them to be versatile actors. Creative Pisceans put their heart in everything—even their food!

MUSHROOM SPELT SAUTÉ

*Compassionate Pisces love a dish that brings them back to their center.
Mushroom Spelt Sauté is a simple, satisfying dish that will bring imaginative
Pisces back down to earth. Spelt is a nutty wheat berry shaped like a
plump grain of rice; it takes a while to cook, but you know it's totally
worth it, whimsical Pisces. Cremini mushrooms are your best bet to
complement the naturally buttery flavor of the spelt, though artistic
Pisceans might like to give it a whirl with white buttons or porcinis.
This dish may seem mellow, but its flavor is otherworldly good.
Pair this with the Pecan Fish with Sweet Potatoes
(see recipe in this chapter) for a dish that wows!*

SERVES 4

2 tablespoons extra-virgin olive oil
1 large onion, peeled and diced
2 cloves garlic, chopped
¼ teaspoon kosher salt, divided
1 (10-ounce package) sliced
   mushrooms

¼ cup dry sherry or white wine
2 cups cooked spelt
⅛ teaspoon ground black pepper

1. Heat olive oil in a medium skillet over high heat until it shimmers and a piece of onion sizzles in it. Add onion and garlic; sprinkle with ⅛ teaspoon salt and cook 5 minutes until onions are translucent.
2. Add mushrooms and cook, stirring occasionally, until some browning occurs, about 5 minutes. Add sherry and cook until it has almost all evaporated, about 2–3 minutes.
3. Add spelt and cook until heated through. Season with remaining salt and pepper and serve.

CORNBALL SOUP

If you've never had Cornball Soup, otherworldly Pisces, this just might be the out-of-this-solar-system food that you've been dreaming of finding. Similar to a matzo ball soup, but from a completely different part of the world, this soup is made of cornmeal and loaded with the bold flavors of garlic, onion, cilantro, and Parmesan. Yes, this soup is exquisitely unique, just like you, extraordinary Pisces. The base of this soup is purposely simple to showcase the lightly fried balls of cornmeal; however, celestial Pisceans will love experimenting with embellishments.

SERVES 8

- 1 small yellow onion, peeled and minced
- 1 clove garlic, minced
- 2 cups masa harina or cornmeal
- 1 cup milk
- 2 large eggs
- ¼ cup freshly grated Parmesan cheese
- 1 teaspoon dried cilantro
- 2 large red tomatoes, cored, peeled, and cut into quarters
- ¼ cup vegetable oil
- 8 cups chicken broth
- 2 teaspoons salt
- 1 teaspoon ground black pepper

1. In a medium bowl, combine onion, garlic, masa harina or cornmeal, milk, eggs, Parmesan cheese, and cilantro. Roll into balls about 1½"–2".
2. Put tomatoes in a blender or food processor and blend on medium setting until thick and creamy.
3. In a medium skillet over medium-high heat, heat vegetable oil. Add cornmeal balls and fry until lightly brown, about 2–3 minutes. (Cut one open to make sure they are cooked into the center.) Keep them warm by putting them in a warm oven.
4. In a large stockpot over medium heat, heat broth. Stir in the tomato purée, salt, and black pepper. Add cornmeal balls. Serve immediately.

BEET GRAPEFRUIT SALAD

Celestial Pisceans will be star struck by the glamour of this citrusy beet salad. If you play your cards right, Pisces, you can glean all your grapefruit ingredients from just one grapefruit rather than two. First, zest the prettiest pink grapefruit you can find; secondly, slice away the rind and bitter white pith. Next, slice perfect grapefruit wedges from between the membranes and allow a bowl to catch the juices for your dressing. See? Your art degree is finally paying off. You detect beauty everywhere, compassionate Pisces, but you'll especially find it in this visually stunning, divinely delicious salad!

SERVES 4

3 large beets with greens
1 medium shallot, peeled and grated
¼ cup sherry vinegar
3 tablespoons extra-virgin olive oil
2 tablespoons fresh grapefruit juice

1½ teaspoons Dijon mustard
½ teaspoon grapefruit zest
2 medium grapefruits, peeled and
  sectioned

1. Preheat oven to 350°F.
2. Chop off beet greens and tear into bite-sized pieces. Set aside.
3. Peel and quarter beets. Arrange beets in a single layer on a baking pan and roast 60 minutes or until tender.
4. Meanwhile, in a small bowl, whisk together shallot, vinegar, oil, grapefruit juice, mustard, and zest. Set aside.
5. Arrange beet greens in a serving bowl or plate. Top with cooked (hot or cold) beets and grapefruit. Drizzle with grapefruit juice dressing and serve.

PECAN FISH WITH SWEET POTATOES

Imaginative Pisces can have their dinner dreams manifested in this delicious one-dish wonder. Sweet potato slices are roasted until soft, while fish fillets are coated with a delectable pecan crust for the perfect amount of texture. With a hint of cayenne pepper, this dish is just enough spicy and sweet for you, Pisces. Free-flowing Pisces will appreciate how easy this dish is to prepare—and since there's only one dish, cleanup is easy too! With plenty to go around, dreamy Pisces can pair this dish with the Mushroom Spelt Sauté (see recipe in this chapter) for an astronomical dinner to share with family or friends!

SERVES 8

4 medium sweet potatoes, peeled and cubed
1 medium onion, peeled and chopped
4 cloves garlic, minced
2 tablespoons olive oil
½ teaspoon salt
¼ teaspoon ground black pepper

½ cup ground pecans
⅓ cup wheat germ
¼ cup whole-wheat flour
⅛ teaspoon cayenne pepper
8 (6-ounce) cod fillets
⅓ cup honey mustard

1. Preheat oven to 400°F.
2. In a large roasting pan, combine sweet potatoes with onion and garlic. Drizzle with olive oil and sprinkle with salt and pepper.
3. Roast 40–45 minutes, turning once with a spatula during roasting time.
4. Meanwhile, on a plate, combine pecans, wheat germ, flour, and cayenne pepper.
5. Coat fish fillets with honey mustard on one side only and then press that side into the pecan mixture.
6. When sweet potatoes are tender, place fish, pecan-side up, on top of them. Roast another 10–15 minutes or until fish flakes when tested with a fork. Serve immediately.

SWEET AND SOUR PORK

Sometimes it's necessary for you to curate your own world and replenish yourself, Pisces. There's nothing you love more than ordering Chinese takeout, watching a long-anticipated movie, and ignoring all incoming texts. This time, you'll be cooking up your own Chinese food! Get ready to amaze yourself at how fast, easy, and sumptuous your own version will turn out to be. Yes, it might even be faster (and more delicious) than takeout. Celestial fish can always use fresh pineapple juice instead of canned. Serve this dish with hot cooked brown rice.

SERVES 8

- 2 pounds boneless pork loin chops, cut into 1" cubes
- ½ teaspoon salt
- ⅛ teaspoon ground black pepper
- 1 (20-ounce) can pineapple tidbits, drained and liquid reserved
- ¼ cup brown sugar
- ½ cup apple cider vinegar
- 2 tablespoons reduced-sodium soy sauce
- 3 tablespoons ketchup
- ¼ teaspoon ground ginger
- 2 tablespoons cornstarch
- 1 tablespoon olive oil
- 1 cup sliced celery
- 1 medium red bell pepper, seeded and chopped
- 1 medium onion, peeled and chopped

1. Sprinkle pork with salt and pepper.
2. In a small bowl, combine 1 cup pineapple liquid, brown sugar, vinegar, soy sauce, ketchup, ginger, and cornstarch. Mix well and set aside.
3. In a large skillet or wok, heat oil over medium heat and add pork; stir-fry until pork is browned, about 5 minutes, and remove from skillet. Add celery, bell pepper, and onion; stir-fry until crisp-tender, about 5 minutes.
4. Return pork to skillet and stir-fry 1 minute. Stir the pineapple liquid mixture and then add to skillet along with pineapple tidbits. Cook and stir until bubbly, then continue cooking, stirring frequently, until pork and vegetables are tender, about 3 minutes more. Serve immediately.

PISTACHIO TEA SANDWICHES

It's a good thing that tea sandwiches are not just for tea parties. These adorable, iconic tiny triangles are always fun to eat at social gatherings, though this recipe offers a deliciously unique twist that enigmatic Pisceans will adore. Crunchy pistachios are folded into an orange-infused cream cheese, along with tiny bites of dried fruit. This little sandwich brings big satisfaction—and that's all you ever want in a party dish, compassionate Pisces! Your two different breads offer your guests variety, so it will be hard for them to eat just one!

SERVES 6

6 ounces cream cheese, softened
2 tablespoons orange juice
⅓ cup chopped pistachios
½ cup chopped dried apricots

¼ cup chopped dried cranberries
6 slices thinly sliced pumpernickel bread
6 slices thinly sliced rye bread

1. In a small bowl, beat cream cheese until fluffy. Add orange juice and beat until smooth. Stir in pistachios, apricots, and cranberries. Set aside.
2. Arrange bread slices on work surface. Spread half of each type of bread with the cream cheese mixture. Top with remaining bread slices, matching types so sandwiches are made with the same variety of bread. Wrap sandwiches in plastic wrap and refrigerate up to 4 hours.
3. When ready to serve, unwrap sandwiches and cut each into four triangles. Arrange on platter and serve.

CRAB RANGOON

Magical Pisces are sure to impress their guests with Crab Rangoon—one of your all-time favorite snacks! Crunchy fried wontons envelop a creamy filling of crabmeat, cream cheese, and green onion. Thoughtful Pisces will get as much satisfaction eating them as they will sharing them with their guests. You're naturally creative and crafty, Pisces, so put on your favorite podcast and lose track of time folding your wontons. Wontons can be kept frozen until you're ready to deep-fry. Serve with your favorite dipping sauce.

YIELDS 48 WONTONS

48 wonton wrappers
1 cup fresh or canned crabmeat
1 cup cream cheese
½ teaspoon Worcestershire sauce
½ teaspoon soy sauce
⅛ teaspoon ground white pepper

2 teaspoons minced onion
1½ medium green onions, thinly sliced
1 large clove garlic, minced
Water, for wetting wontons
4 cups oil, for deep-frying

1. Cover wonton wrappers with a damp towel to prevent drying. Set aside.
2. In a large bowl, flake crabmeat with a fork (if using canned crabmeat, drain it thoroughly first). Add cream cheese and mix to combine. Then mix in Worcestershire sauce, soy sauce, white pepper, onion, green onions, and garlic.
3. Lay a wrapper in a diamond shape or circle, depending on the shape of wonton wrappers you are using. Add a heaping teaspoon of filling in the middle; spread out evenly but not too near the edges.
4. Using your clean finger, spread water along all four sides. Fold up the middle of two opposite sides until they meet. Squeeze lightly together. Bring the middle of the two other sides together and lightly squeeze to close the wonton. Gently squeeze to seal wonton. Cover filled wontons with a damp towel to prevent drying.
5. Heat oil in a 16" preheated wok to 375°F.
6. Slide wontons in a few at a time and deep-fry 2–3 minutes until they turn golden brown.
7. Remove with a slotted spoon and drain on paper towels. Cool and serve.

MINI BAKLAVA APRICOT CHEESECAKES

Is there anything on this earth more magical than cheesecake? Doubtful. Cheesecake's signature creamy fluffiness transports these celestial fishes' senses to the stars. Whimsical Pisces will get a kick out of these miniature muffin-sized cheesecakes with a sumptuous baklava flair.

SERVES 12

2 (8-ounce) packages cream cheese, softened
¾ cup granulated sugar
1 large egg
2 large egg whites
¼ cup orange juice
1 teaspoon vanilla extract
2 tablespoons butter, melted

3 tablespoons honey
6 (9" × 14") sheets frozen phyllo dough, thawed
¼ cup ground walnuts
1 (15-ounce) can apricot halves, drained and coarsely chopped
¾ cup apricot jam

1. Preheat oven to 350°F.
2. In a large bowl, combine cream cheese with sugar and beat until smooth. Add egg, egg whites, orange juice, and vanilla and beat until smooth and creamy. Set aside.
3. In a small bowl, combine butter with honey and mix well.
4. Arrange a sheet of phyllo dough on work surface and brush with the butter mixture; sprinkle with 1 tablespoon walnuts. Add another sheet of phyllo and layer again with butter and walnuts. Top with another phyllo sheet.
5. Cut the phyllo stack into six squares by cutting in half to make two 4½" × 14" rectangles, then cutting each rectangle into thirds. Gently press into muffin cups. Repeat with remaining three sheets of phyllo dough, the butter mixture, and walnuts.
6. Spoon the cream cheese mixture into each lined muffin cup. Bake 16–20 minutes or until filling is just set. Cool completely.
7. In a medium bowl, combine chopped apricots with apricot jam. Top each cooled cheesecake with this mixture. Chill 2–3 hours before serving.

JELLY ROLL

*Your second-favorite dessert? Without a doubt, sponge cake!
This time your beloved sponge cake shape-shifts into a delightful Jelly Roll.
Sure to bring you cheer, magical Pisces, this classic dessert is sweet in all
the right ways. Do you have to have a jelly roll pan? If not, a regular baking
pan will work fine as long as it's covered in parchment paper. Imaginative
Pisceans can flex their creative muscles in the jam department. Quince jam?
Elderberry preserves? Rambutan? You're unafraid to reach for
sweet rarities, unique Pisces. Because that's how you roll.*

SERVES 10

⅔ cup all-purpose flour
1 teaspoon baking powder
¼ teaspoon salt
4 large eggs, separated

¾ cup granulated sugar, divided
1½ teaspoons vanilla extract
8 ounces jam

1. Preheat oven to 375°F. Grease a jelly roll pan. Line pan with parchment paper and grease again.
2. In a large bowl, whisk together flour, baking powder, and salt. Set aside.
3. In a medium bowl, whisk yolks together until yellow and creamy. Add ½ cup sugar in a steady stream and beat until well mixed. Stir in vanilla. Slowly stream into the flour mixture until incorporated.
4. In another large mixing bowl, beat egg whites with an electric mixer until soft peaks form. Gradually add remaining sugar. Continue beating until stiff peaks form. Fold egg whites into the batter.
5. Pour the batter into prepared pan. Bake 12–15 minutes or until golden and spongy to the touch.
6. Turn the cake over onto a towel. Peel off the parchment paper, then roll the cake and towel together tightly, starting with the narrow end. Allow to cool to room temperature.
7. Unroll and spread with jam. Re-roll and slice with a bread or serrated cake knife.

BLUE HAWAIIAN

Mystical Pisceans seek a magical cocktail that can transport their senses to some faraway land. Preferably the beach. That's why celestial Pisceans will be enamored by the tropical Blue Hawaiian. This hypnotic blue-hued cocktail gets its cosmic flair from curaçao, a liqueur with an (ironically) orangey flavor. Pisceans adore a sweet spirit such as rum, and especially so in a Blue Hawaiian. Sweet in all the right ways, this blue cocktail is otherworldly enough to pique your interest, enigmatic Pisces, so swim up to your own barstool and stir it up.

SERVES 1

1 ounce light rum
1 ounce blue curaçao

Pineapple juice to fill
1 pineapple slice

Pour the liquid ingredients into a highball glass of ice. Stir and garnish with pineapple slice.

Standard US/Metric Measurement Conversions

VOLUME CONVERSIONS

US Volume Measure	Metric Equivalent
⅛ teaspoon	0.5 milliliter
¼ teaspoon	1 milliliter
½ teaspoon	2 milliliters
1 teaspoon	5 milliliters
½ tablespoon	7 milliliters
1 tablespoon (3 teaspoons)	15 milliliters
2 tablespoons (1 fluid ounce)	30 milliliters
¼ cup (4 tablespoons)	60 milliliters
⅓ cup	90 milliliters
½ cup (4 fluid ounces)	125 milliliters
⅔ cup	160 milliliters
¾ cup (6 fluid ounces)	180 milliliters
1 cup (16 tablespoons)	250 milliliters
1 pint (2 cups)	500 milliliters
1 quart (4 cups)	1 liter (about)

WEIGHT CONVERSIONS

US Weight Measure	Metric Equivalent
½ ounce	15 grams
1 ounce	30 grams
2 ounces	60 grams
3 ounces	85 grams
¼ pound (4 ounces)	115 grams
½ pound (8 ounces)	225 grams
¾ pound (12 ounces)	340 grams
1 pound (16 ounces)	454 grams

OVEN TEMPERATURE CONVERSIONS

Degrees Fahrenheit	Degrees Celsius
200 degrees F	95 degrees C
250 degrees F	120 degrees C
275 degrees F	135 degrees C
300 degrees F	150 degrees C
325 degrees F	160 degrees C
350 degrees F	180 degrees C
375 degrees F	190 degrees C
400 degrees F	205 degrees C
425 degrees F	220 degrees C
450 degrees F	230 degrees C

BAKING PAN SIZES

American	Metric
8 x 1½ inch round baking pan	20 x 4 cm cake tin
9 x 1½ inch round baking pan	23 x 3.5 cm cake tin
11 x 7 x 1½ inch baking pan	28 x 18 x 4 cm baking tin
13 x 9 x 2 inch baking pan	30 x 20 x 5 cm baking tin
2 quart rectangular baking dish	30 x 20 x 3 cm baking tin
15 x 10 x 2 inch baking pan	30 x 25 x 2 cm baking tin (Swiss roll tin)
9 inch pie plate	22 x 4 or 23 x 4 cm pie plate
7 or 8 inch springform pan	18 or 20 cm springform or loose bottom cake tin
9 x 5 x 3 inch loaf pan	23 x 13 x 7 cm or 2 lb narrow loaf or pâté tin
1½ quart casserole	1.5 liter casserole
2 quart casserole	2 liter casserole

Index